Spirit of the

ZAMBEZI

Jeff & Veronica Stutchbury

Spirit of the
ZAMBEZI

ISBN Nº 0-9515209-2-X

Publisher
CBC Publishing
36 Finborough Road
London SW10 9EG

Design
Copyright © Mick Pilcher 1992
Pilcher Graphics Limited
PO Box 30806, Lusaka 10101 Zambia
and
Barney Wan, London

Colour separations, printing and binding
Craft Print Pte Ltd
9 Joo Koon Circle, Singapore 2262

Acknowledgements

The Stutchbury family promised Jeff that they would finish the job he started and publish this book. Many dear friends contributed to this effort in many different ways. To them all, our sincere thanks. Particular mention should be made of:

Jill Day for her words.

John Edlin and Mick Pilcher for their professional skill.

Russell and Lyn Taylor for scientific verification.

Marilyn Dawson for hours of agonising over upper and lower case, italics or plain and for tempering my sometimes too direct text.

Clive Wilson for being an editor's editor.

Mary Ashton for handling Jeff's photographs over the years.

Jennifer Allen, Lesley Malkin and Helen Maxwell for their hard work.

Dick Dawson for final proof reading and tolerance when we invaded his home and monopolised his machine.

Gerry Jackson and Joy Koster for keeping us sane when it seemed impossible, and to our publisher Ian Murphy.

And lastly, we wish fond memories to the authors of the fine tributes to Jeff.

Dedication

To our sons Ralph, Glenn and Wayne.

We commit to you the pursuit of dreams and hatching of schemes.

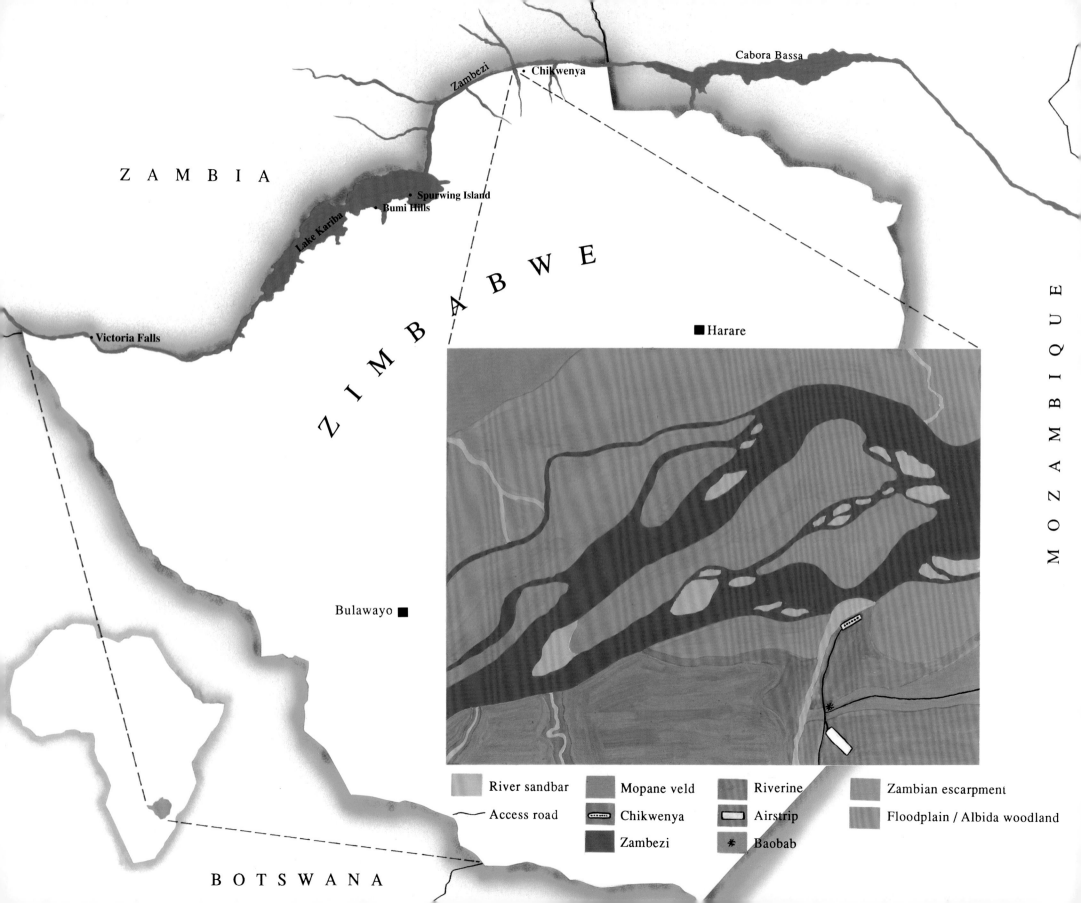

ZAMBIA

Zambezi • Chikwenya

Cabora Bassa

• Spurwing Island
• Bumi Hills

Lake Kariba

• Victoria Falls

ZIMBABWE

■ Harare

MOZAMBIQUE

Bulawayo ■

BOTSWANA

	River sandbar		Mopane veld		Riverine		Zambian escarpment
	Access road		Chikwenya		Airstrip		Floodplain / Albida woodland
	Zambezi		Baobab				

Preface

Few people are lucky enough to live and work in such an area as the wild and unspoiled Zambezi Valley. This magnificent wilderness has been our home for over thirty years. We kept our minds, eyes and ears open and this is our story of the wild creatures and untouched places that we love.

We cannot just take, we must give back and this is our willing contribution. We invite you to share our experience; shed tears with us, laugh and rejoice, but never allow your passion to cool, become subdued or die.

The photographs are a statement by Jeff of beautiful moments which nature offers to those privileged enough to experience the 'Spirit of the Zambezi'. This is his invitation, 'Come with me', he is saying. 'Let me show you what I have found'.

Life on the lake

In the beginning ...

In the beginning we were valley dwellers. For thirty years our lives have been inextricably tied to the Zambezi River. We lived and worked on the north bank of the river during the time of the Federation of Rhodesia and Nyasaland, when Jeff was employed by the Northern Rhodesian Game Department.

We had just married and I moved from Lusaka to join Jeff at the Game and Tsetse station at Mzimbe, some fifteen kilometres upstream from Chirundu. Our home was what I always thought of as 'the house of singing bamboo'. It was built almost entirely of a local river reed, *Phragmites*, which we called *matetti*. Above all, it was different from standard houses which have doors, windows, and solid walls and rooms all on one level and it was cool and looked natural. Jeff had been married before and Ralph, his son, became mine too. I was very happy about this but I believe that sometimes, Ralph, who had been living a very free life,

Strong, dramatic sunsets are a feature of the lake and each evening offers another opportunity for avid photographers to capture the splendour.

resented the order I attempted to introduce. After one weekend visit just before our marriage I left to return to Lusaka for work on Monday. But I left late, drove too fast on the rough bush track in my Morris Minor and hit a large rock, which broke the sump. In my ignorance I continued to drive until the engine seized. Two alternatives were available. Either I could stay in the car till morning and then walk back, or I could begin to walk back immediately. I opted for the latter course, reasoning that the sooner I got back to the camp, the sooner something could be done. Happily the moon was rising and the road was clearly defined but I was mightily relieved, when about fifteen kilometres later, I saw 'the house of singing bamboo', with the river gleaming beyond. I bleated, 'Jeff, Jeff ... ' and he eventually woke up and I heard Ralph say to his Dad, 'I thought she had gone!' He must have had visions of having to clean his teeth properly all over again.

Kariba Dam

Life in the valley during the Federation period was altered for all time. The momentous event of the period as far we were concerned was the decision to dam the Zambezi River, and the building of Kariba Dam has had an overwhelming impact on our lives. The construction of the dam was necessary to provide greater quantities of electricity for the industrial and agricultural expansion planned in the surrounding countries. The inhospitable and wild geography of the Zambezi Valley presented an extraordinary challenge both to the engineers constructing the dam and to the conservationists left with the altered environment.

The rugged terrain, characterised by the steep escarpment, coupled with the severe climate of the valley, involved surveyors and engineers in great feats of ingenuity as they built access roads, airports and housing as well as the dam wall itself. The initial access road on the south bank was amazing. The escarpment through which the approach to the dam wall had to be made was formidable, raising doubts as to the feasibility of constructing a suitable road. The engineer's clever solution was simply to follow the elephant trails, which utilised gradient and less precipitous declines, in the masterful ways of these beasts.

As well as ingenuity, the engineer also had some romance in his soul, and he and his team made signposts on the road such as Buffalo Nek, Puff Adder Ridge and Savory's Folly. It was sad that in 1966, when the road was tarred and straightened, all those signs were also removed. The road is now much easier to negotiate, but is also relatively dull and uninteresting by comparison.

Operation Noah

Further unusual plans were devised by the small and untrained team of men who were initially the task force responsible for mounting 'Operation Noah', the game rescue programme. Their dedicated and often herculean efforts saved huge numbers of stranded animals from the flood waters of the rising dam and gave inspiration to many a young person who cared about wild things and wild places.

Although the construction of the dam was a Federal responsibility the game rescue programmes were handled independently by the game departments of Northern and Southern Rhodesia. In the south the driving force was Rupert Fothergill, after whom Fothergill Island is named, whilst the team on the north bank was led by Tad Edelman. Jeff assisted on a number of occasions, as did all members of the Game Department.

By far the greater number of endangered animals were on the southern side of the rapidly rising lake. This was due to the very different geographical features of the two sides of the river. In the south, a second large river gorge, the Sanyati, rises very steep sided and high. The mountainous terrain of the combined river gorges created far more temporary islands with stranded game needing rescue, than amongst the relatively flat land with more shallow rises which characterised the northern banks of the newly formed lake. Most of the animals from the southern islands were moved to an area on the mainland which was then the Matusadona Game Reserve but which was reclassified as a national park in 1975.

With the creation of Lake Kariba the focus of work for the Game Department moved from the valley to the lake and so

Kariba's drowned trees whose bare branches host birds, insects and even reptiles. The banks of kariba weed, Salvinia molesta, which collect in the protected creeks, support a mini ecosystem, illustrating the complexity of the lake's continuing development.

we had to move, unwillingly at first, to Gwena on the lakeshore, about fifteen kilometres by water from the village of Siavonga. Our misgivings about living on the lake were unfounded and it was a most rewarding time as we lived with and observed the development of a new lake ecosystem.

One of my most vivid memories of that time was the oh-so-strange feeling of boating in an area, which just last week, had been dry land. We floated amongst a forest of mopane trees, all with their canopy of green leaves intact. The hardwoods stood up to the advancing waters but the softwoods and shallow-rooted trees soon collapsed. What an experience it was for us to suddenly come upon a giant baobab floating freely, blown to and fro by the wind. Our small, open fibreglass boat did not give a great feeling of security when we were about to be rammed by this leviathan, often still acting as host to a number of smaller mammals and reptiles. The baobabs peeled off, layer by layer, as the water permeated their soft, fibrous bark and they disintegrated.

Kariba weed and the grasshoppers

Another very strong recollection I have of those early days of the lake is of the battles we had with the vast stretches of *Salvinia molesta,* which soon came to be commonly known as Kariba weed. This free-floating aquatic plant attained a dangerous level of success and at one stage in the early 1960s some twenty five per cent of the lake's surface was covered in weedbanks. The salvinia is not indigenous to Africa, originating in South America, but the nutrient-rich waters of the newly formed lake provided an ideal combination of climate and food and the weed spread like wildfire. Huge floating islands were soon to be seen carrying with them self-contained populations of birds and insects and giving shelter to numerous species of fish. It was felt that the volume of weed cover was potentially dangerous and so the scientists set about trying to devise a method of control.

One idea which was tried, was to import a weed-eating grasshopper called *Paulinia* from South America, the home of the weed itself. Experiments were made with the grasshopper at the research station at Sinamwenda, under controlled conditions. It was inevitable that some of the fast-growing population of *Paulinia* would escape, and they provided a veritable feast for the lake birds of all shapes and sizes. So *Paulinia* did not make much progress in controlling the weed but the birds apparently controlled the numbers of the unlucky grasshopper. Eventually the lake surface covered by the weed decreased to approximately one per cent due to natural controls in the form of wave action, which isolated the weed mats, combined with the reduced nutrient levels in the waters of the lake. This effectively cut down the volume of weed almost to the stage when lake scientists were concerned that

there was too little weed to support its mini ecosystem, as opposed to the lake being overrun with it.

However, in the lake's early days, the weed growth would often completely block off the more protected bays and lagoons. Sometimes, when Jeff had to organize a patrol into a specific area which could not be reached by land, we would approach these bays equipped with pieces of polystyrene which the men would throw onto the weedbanks. They would then flop ashore using the polystyrene rafts to disperse their weight. From the shelter of the boat, and as an interested observer only, I was provided with many a giggle as it presented such a contrast to the 'starched shorts, polished boots and sharp snappy salute', which was the usual image of the game scouts.

The formation of the lake naturally caused major changes in the habitat and the end-result in scientific terms provided previously unrivalled opportunities for research to the botanists, zoologists and ichthyologists. The settling down period was of great interest to the layman too, especially with regard to the development of a new and more supportive ecosystem. This was most evident along the Matusadona shoreline where the barren sandstone was gradually covered with a lush growth of *Panicum repens*, a form of torpedo grass which colonized the shoreline, benefiting from the mulching effect of the mats of salvinia stranded there when the lake levels fluctuated.

With the break up of the Federation in 1963, Jeff and I left the Game Department and Northern Rhodesia in search of something different, exciting and challenging to do. Not at that stage having very many responsibilities, we embarked on a series of ventures such as attempting to grow burley tobacco on the outskirts of Salisbury, opening up and developing a banana farm at Charara on the shores of Lake Kariba and catching crocodiles for the Kariba Crocodile Farm. However our responsibilities grew with the arrival of two more sons. Glenn arrived in December 1965 and Wayne was born in November 1968 and we felt that we should perhaps attempt something which might yield a more secure income. So we went to Wankie Game Park to work for a company which held a concession on all three camps. This proved to be a good move from one point of view, as we learned a lot more about game species with which we had not been familiar when living in the Zambezi Valley, but the lure of the lake was very strong and so in 1971 we returned to our preferred habitat.

The tent camps of Kariba

In the early 1970s, a spinoff from the main objective of supplying power was the development of the tourist industry on the lake. We decided to become involved in that tourist development. Our first foray into the commercial field, Camera Africa Safaris, was in the form of a tented camp on the shores of Lake Kariba in the Matusadona National Park. Over the years we had become aware of the great potential of the Matusadona and at that stage we were pioneers, so to speak, as there were no other tourist operations so far afield. We were very enthusiastic, excited and eager to explore the potential of this undeveloped natural paradise. We were also very wet behind the ears, as was our partner Robin Hughes. None of us had had any relevant commercial experience at all. Robin had been with the Rhodesian Department of National

Although the primary reason for the building of Kariba Dam was to provide electricity, other industries developed as spinoffs. Crocodile farming is one secondary use of the lake's resource. The butter-coloured flap at the back of the mouth seals the throat of the reptile, enabling it to take prey underwater, and also acts as a temperature control, in that light colours reflect heat.

Parks for ten years and, like me was African born and bred. Jeff was originally a 'Brit', but rather like a convert to a religion, his feeling for Africa was strong and intense and grew increasingly deep-seated.

Tourists were only just beginning to realize the enormous potential of Lake Kariba and our small, unknown, tented camp did not attract vast numbers of visitors, although those who did manage to find us most certainly enjoyed exploring the untouched wilderness areas. However, common sense prevailed and we decided to establish a permanent base camp from which to operate.

Spurwing Island

The acquisition of land for such an operation was not easy but eventually we secured a lease on Spurwing Island, approximately twenty kilometres from the village of Kariba across the lake, and just west of the Sanyati Gorge. Finances were fairly acute at that time and I used to regularly disappear back to town to work for a few months, providing finance which helped us to survive long enough to establish a home on Spurwing.

Ralph at this time was at boarding school and I was teaching the two younger boys by correspondence until they were old enough to join him. One particular incident relating to our island 'school', remains very vividly in my mind. Glenn's nature project involved finding and observing the

Bank erosion causes trees to collapse into the river providing ideal nesting sites for spottedbacked weavers.

14

construction of a bird's nest. He found the nest of a tawny flanked prinia and each day we checked on the progress: building complete ... eggs laid ... eggs hatched ... , and then disaster! No nest at all! It had been built in a short scrub mopane bush and the branch *in toto* had been browsed by a buffalo during the night. He was, naturally, quite distraught, but 'Nature Study' had taught him something about natural laws and this was no doubt his first lesson in the loss of life.

'Home' was very basic. First of all we had just three tents and a mess tent. The kitchen was the traditional fireplace consisting of three flat stones and the shower was provided by using a twenty litre tin on a rope and a pulley! When it was shower-time the staff lowered the bucket, filled it up with hot water and pulled it up ready for the guests' use. Generally it worked well but there were occasions when there would be a call from the naked and vulnerable guest behind the grass fence, 'Please can you lower the bucket? I can't reach the tap!' This was a direct result of my having given strict instructions that it was to be pulled up to its limits in order that *I* could avoid having my head knocked off by the wildly swinging tin of hot water. The staff found it difficult to get a happy medium to cope with my two metre body and the average guest! I also suffered from a bit of over-exposure with regard to the height of the fence around the 'shower'. The builder had not taken into account my length of leg so initially when I took a shower in daytime I had to be very conscious of keeping my knees bent!

It was on Spurwing Island that Jeff first developed his specialised watercraft for game-viewing and photography. He experimented with various combinations eventually deciding

that the ultimately supreme, steady, photographic platform was to be achieved by linking three canoe hulls with a light decking. The engine was mounted on the centre hull and he developed a unique steering method using a bar which was operated by foot, leaving both hands free to use binoculars and cameras. The trick with this type of craft is to remember that if you push your left leg forward you will go left, rather like reversing a trailer.

One of my most embarrassing moments resulted from trying to operate the trimaran when it was brand new. A hydrofoil used to make trips up and down the lake and it also made day trips to the Sanyati Gorge. Sometimes our guests would take the hydrofoil to the gorge and then get 'dropped

Jeff's first pontoon boat was called Nakapakapa which means pied kingfisher. The rationale behind this name was that pied kingfishers hover and plummet into the water when fishing, and although Nakapakapa did not exactly hover, she always popped up again, even in the heavy swells when crossing the Ume River mouth in order to reach the peaceful waters of the Chura River.

off' for their visit to Spurwing. Because the foils drew a considerable depth of water it was impossible for the vessel to come right into harbour so we used to go out in one of the small boats to collect visitors. On one occasion, as I was the only person left on the island, I had to make the pick-up from the hydrofoil. I had not yet attempted to drive the trimaran, but no other boat was available! What a performance it turned out to be. I just could not synchronise my eyes and my feet, and literally went round in ever decreasing circles. In desperation, I knelt on the deck and managed, by using my hands to push the rudder bar, to approach the stern of the hydrofoil. Humiliated, I tied up and assisted the obviously nervous guests onto the deck of this apparently dubiously designed craft. Having accomplished this, all I wanted was to reach the safety of our harbour as quickly as possible, but with my complete inexperience further mortification was in store for me, as I kept overcompensating and we proceeded over the water in a series of lurches to right and left! Camera Africa Safaris extended its operation by offering drives, walks and cruises in Mana Pools National Park. Robin was in charge of this as he had been a ranger in the Zambezi Valley, knew it intimately and so was the perfect choice of guide. His outstanding ability was to communicate naturally with the game scouts in their own languages. He had a rare understanding of their traditional beliefs and was something of an authority on Chimombe, the Iron God, believed to inhabit the Chewore region.

Back at Spurwing, Jeff's inventiveness extended further and he had developed his widely-copied design for a double storey thatched bar and dining area. He then went on to build a couple of truly marvellous tree platforms in the waters along the shoreline of the Matusadona National Park. These were lovely for spending the night in at full moon, but sadly that aspect of use soon had to be curtailed as the area was becoming more and more affected by the civil war which was intensifying.

The tourist industry was in a state of decline, due to political uncertainty, and although we had by this stage made great progress with buildings, basically there was no-one to enjoy these facilities. Guests were just not prepared to visit what was considered to be, in the parlance of the times, a 'hot' area. We were vulnerable as we were situated on the border with Zambia. We, of course, did not see it in quite that way. After all, we reasoned, we had the width of the lake between us. However there were curfews, convoys and the regular call-ups of all the able-bodied men to cope with. I was often left alone on the island with our two younger sons as Jeff had joined the 'Water Wing' of the Police Reserve and did call-ups regularly. Robin, our partner, was an accomplished tracker and an extraordinary bushman. These skills were increasingly required during the bush war and eventually he was seconded into the National Parks Tracker Unit. Whilst he was on an active follow up he was ambushed and killed. His death meant that we not only lost a partner in our venture, but also a very dear friend. The lack of tourists was, I suppose, not unreasonable. The total absence of capital reserves meant that we were forced to give up Spurwing Island and seek employment elsewhere.

The floating safari camp

Thankfully, we accepted the position of managers of Bumi Hills Safari Lodge and during the following seven years gained a great deal of knowledge and a certain degree of expertise. Whilst at Bumi Hills, Jeff took the opportunities which abounded for someone with vision and again made his mark all over the shoreline with thatched double storey game-viewing platforms as well as bigger and better boats for photographic forays into the unknown and unexplored bays of the Ume River.

He also conceived what many people at the time considered foolish, but was a masterful idea. The Water Wilderness Safari concept was both an extension of his photographic platform and the safari camp rolled into one. The magical part of Water Wilderness was that both elements of the safari were on the water giving an added dimension to the experience. A totally water-orientated safari base camp was unheard of and was such a departure from the tried and tested methods that it did cause a few raised eyebrows, but happily there were other men of vision and the project was approved and subsequently proved to be a huge success. The design, construction and operation of Water Wilderness gave Jeff immense satisfaction, as not only was he doing something different, but again he was doing it in an area which was almost untouched, namely on the Ume River and the Chura Bay where the craft were moored.

Places closer to Kariba were becoming, by our standards, over-populated and crowded with other vessels but initially the

At Water Wilderness, the mother ship tied up to the platform and meals were served on the first level under thatch. The protected waters of the Chura Bay created reflections as sharp as 'the real thing'.

remoteness, together with the formidable tree-line behind which we operated, meant that our safaris were undisturbed, uninterrupted and unparalleled. The lake reached its highest-ever level and we took advantage of the high water to explore many of the previously unknown creeks and river beds. We ventured into some enchanting lagoons and protected bays where good numbers of black rhinoceros were to be found. It was here too, that Jeff found the Chura Bull, a magnificent elephant specimen, still roaming the shores of Matusadona and carrying enormous and graceful tusks. We learned that he died in 1991 as a result of wounds inflicted by a younger and more agile bull. Chura Bull's magnificent tusks were unwieldy and were his undoing. However, the day before his death, he had been seen with a breeding herd and we feel sure that his genes will crop up in future generations of Matusadona elephants.

At that time poaching was not the huge problem it has become today, but we still used to worry that this grand old man would cross over the Ume River into the controlled hunting area in the Omay Communal Land. National Parks staff sometimes collared particularly good specimens of elephant and this collar gave them much greater protection as registered hunting safari operators would lose their licences if they allowed any of their clients to shoot a collared animal. But poachers do not play by such rules, so the collar is not much use today when the poachers are so active and deadly.

With the welcome end of hostilities and the advent of peace, the tourist depression was over. More and more people were visiting Zimbabwe and the lake and although we appreciated the financial relief that the increase in tourism provided, we both felt the need to escape to less populous and more remote regions.

During our years on Kariba we had successfully created a growing tourist interest. This now became unacceptable, for it prevented us realising our dream of discovering the secrets of still more wild and uninhabited places. Our operations, now so well-known, were responsible for bringing to the Matusadona more people, boats and vehicles. We were compelled to seek out more remote areas to realise our dreams and decided once again to return to the Zambezi Valley.

Enthusiastic game spotters went to the top level to use the open viewing platform, which gave a grand overview of the Chura River and the surrounding creeks and gulleys. The entire structure was built in the water, using seasoned gum poles in conjunction with the anchor tree, always a hard wood, such as Combretum imberbe, the leadwood.

Overleaf: *Impala constantly seem to be seeking food and are often seen at last light still browing the albida pods which have fallen due to high winds or have, perhaps, been left over by the elephants or baboons.*

Return to the valley

Welcome home

In 1984 Jeff and I returned to the Zambezi Valley and a smaller, more intimate safari operation. We had reacquainted ourselves with the river and the Chikwenya area while on a canoe trip in 1982 and knew that this was the right place for us. It was the ultimate wilderness area. It also seemed right, even vital, that we return to the valley, as Robin's presence in the area in years gone by, was tangible and welcome. One of his signposts still remains at the junction of our airstrip road and the 'G' camp road. It is faded, but visible.

The canoe trip reinforced our determination to return to the valley. It also provided us with a few hilarious moments. The best of these came about as a result of Jeff's persistently paddling too close to the banks, in spite of the guide's advice. The reason for not paddling too close, especially in the early morning, is that it sometimes results in eyeball to eyeball moments with hippos who are returning to water after their night's inland grazing.

Hippo are plentiful in the Zambezi River and it is impossible to avoid the occasional too-close-for comfort encounter. Hippo have the reputation of being responsible for the greatest number of deaths by wild animals in Africa as a whole, so we always treat them with respect.

We were just two canoes. I was in front with the guide, while Jeff and a friend of many years' standing were behind. They were usually too far behind for safety, due to their mutual preoccupation with photography. It was early morning and cool, crisp and quiet. The quiet was not to last long however, as we heard loud, heavy footsteps approaching at speed. The next thing we saw was a 'flying hippo' who flung himself off a two metre high bank between the two canoes with a flourish which almost caused us to flounder in the resultant waves. We had obviously disturbed him, and there was no easy, shallow entry available. In desperation he performed this amazingly athletic feat with precision. He 'flew' over the edge of the bank, having poised himself for just a moment whilst he seemed to assess his chances of missing both craft. Jeff had visions of all his precious photographic equipment disappearing into the Zambezi and so for the next day or two he did heed all the guide's advice.

Valley territory

Chikwenya lies downstream of the Mana Pools National Park, at the point where the Sapi River, a seasonal river which flows only in the rains, joins the Zambezi River. In the Zambezi, opposite the Chikwenya camp lies Chikwenya Island. This land was severed from the mainland in the 1930s by the power of floodwaters which used to rush downstream before man interfered by damming the river at Kariba. It is wild territory, compared to the lake we left behind, and it suited our need for escape and our desire to return to what we consider our 'natural' habitat.

Felt by many who knew the area to be one of the most inhospitable regions of our country, it had escaped lightly when development first began. The climate is harsh and

Left: The Zambezi River, inexorably pushes its way through the side channels and around islands, making and moving sandbars, while it heads steadily for the Indian Ocean. Sights such as this make the blood quicken and the feet begin to itch. The urge to follow the river, through the wilderness to the sea, is very strong.

Individual hippo, hippo families and huge pods (the name for a large group of hippo), due to their density in the river act as stop signs.

Crocodiles have existed for many thousands of years in their present form and are a link with prehistory. In common with all other predators they are opportunists. When living around crocodiles, it is better not to become a creature of habit and use the same stretch of water each day, as they will certainly watch and wait. Their basic diet is fish and as they get bigger they will take small mammals.

the quality of life, measured by today's more materialistic standards, is poor. The local people certainly did not enjoy what most would consider an easy life. However, I believe the early inhabitants of the region were strongly influenced by the power of the river and were proud to be a part of such a supremely wild, remote and rugged environment.

Small numbers of the Tonga people had lived there in simple villages along the river bank. They fished, hunted and cultivated the alluvial soils on the floodplains. Their crops were often destroyed by game and their canoes were attacked by hippos during fishing expeditions. Crocodiles presented an eternal hazard, particularly to the women when they collected water or did their washing by hand at the water's edge. Malaria was rife in the Zambezi Valley and the presence of the tsetse fly prevented the villagers keeping any livestock. Tsetse fly will feed freely on all game species, which do not contract the disease trypanosomiasis, sleeping sickness, but merely act as hosts. However, if domestic stock, such as cattle or goats or pigs, are brought into a tsetse-infected area, they soon fall ill and die from the dreaded *nagana*.

Conserve or destroy

At the time that Kariba Dam was filling, different policies were adopted by the countries on the two sides of the Zambezi. The Southern Rhodesian Government decided that the entire valley from the dam wall to the border with Portuguese East Africa, now Mozambique, would be designated as part of the nation's wildlife estate. This decision was an extension of the policy for the lakeside land. The same kind of plans, made for the resettlement of the tribespeople who were living in the areas to be flooded by the rising waters of Lake Kariba, were needed for the relocation of the Tonga living in this part of the valley.

The number of small communities was not high, as the area had never been densely populated and the people living in the valley were moved to new homes on the escarpment. This policy resulted in the protection of a unique wildlife and wilderness area which, in 1988, was granted World Heritage status. The wildlife estate now consists of controlled hunting areas, hunting concessions, photographic concessions and the well-known Mana Pools National Park.

It is often very unwise to return to a place one has loved and we certainly do love the valley. Had we returned to Zambia and seen the northern bank of the river we would have been in utter despair. No policy of wild life protection in any form had been established. The local population had been left to continue their precarious subsistence existence. Dramatic changes to the habitat had occurred, caused by the wholesale removal of riverine forests and there was horrific evidence of large-scale erosion resulting from the practice of river bank cultivation. Huge, barren areas of land ran adjacent to the river bank, devoid of vegetation, and each year more of the land washed away by the force of the river. The people there still struggled to survive as the quality of the soil is marginal and it should not have been used for agricultural purposes.

The strong attitude of the Department of National Parks of Rhodesia often led to the directorate being accused of having a miserly attitude, so loth were they to allow commercial development and utilisation. The policy of hoarding the natural resources of a country and attempting to keep them pristine is counter-productive today and most people now accept the view that 'if you don't use it you lose it'. So regulations pertaining to the fast growing tourist industry have been relaxed and this has encouraged the flow of visitors in more recent years. Now more people enjoy the grandeur of the Zambezi Valley and the tranquillity of the magnificent river .

The entire region had been closed to all non-military personnel for eight years due to the civil war and in 1982 it was reopened. The Mana Pools National Park itself remained much as it had been, but there was a change in policy and two small photographic concessions were designated. Rukomechi on the western boundary, and Chikwenya, to the east. These were effectively buffers between the safari hunting areas and the national park itself. This development was part of the relaxing of attitudes by the Department of National Parks as to how the land should be used and has, I believe, served a dual purpose. We protect the park from poachers by our presence and daily walks and drives, as do the hunters. We are specialist operators and offer to visitors a bush experience of depth and interest. Our guests benefit from an intensive service as well as intelligent guidance and instruction. This makes them, in many cases, want to return to Zimbabwe and to Chikwenya.

The view from the furthermost point of our concession area. Clumps of Vetevaria still hold out, even though by the end of the dry weather it is a coarse and unpalatable grass eaten only as a last resort by the wild animals. Clouds build up as the wet season approaches, adding an extra dimension to the panorama and giving hope of rain.

The place of the claw marks

The safari camp was named after Chief Chikwenya, as was the island, and was part of his domain in the years prior to the initial exploration of the valley by hunters such as Selous, during the late 1800s. We are told that the name Chikwenya means 'the place of the claw marks' or 'scratching place' and we assume that it was a heavy predator area in those times, unless it was the chief who was scratchy!

Our safari concession is part of the Sapi Safari Area. Most of this area is set aside for the use of sport hunters but our concession is strictly for photographic, game-viewing and walking safaris. It is a small area, relatively speaking, but abounds in such a variety of diverse habitats that it is unusual for us to stray out of our own patch. Immediately adjacent to the river we have rich grassy plains which have formed in the last eight years due to the lack of annual floods and the consequent siltation of the Sapi estuary. Across the Sapi from camp there is a floodplain dotted with *Acacia albida,* the winter thorn or apple-ring trees. This tree has recently been

reclassified and is now called *Faidherbia albida*, but to us it will always be albida.

The Sapi is a rainy season river only, so usually we look across the wide, sandy river bed to the floodplain, beyond which is the Zambezi, Chikwenya Island and, in the mid-distance, the Zambian escarpment. These dry river beds are very much a part of the valley terrain, but cause confusion to guests from overseas who naturally expect a river to have water. The floodplains always seem to be colonised first by albidas, and then other trees such as the evergreen *Trichelia emetica*, Natal mahogany, develop. So, as we look, the airy, light bluish-green of the albidas contrasts strongly with the occasional, dark green, solid trichelias.

The area is littered with termite mounds and they all point towards the prevailing wind. This, I am told, is so the millions of inhabitants have a form of air conditioning. The air flow helps to keep the temperature of the termitaria constant. Riverine vegetation and thick clay soils exist along the banks of the Sapi and this habitat is ideal for kudu and bushbuck, as well as the more secretive nyala antelope.

The soil changes dramatically once we get near the airstrip and we find a band of very acidic soil which supports *Hypheane benguellensis*, the northern ilala palms, scrub mopane and *Adansonia digitata,* the baobab. It is here that we see the biggest and best of these grand, ancient baobabs. It is marginally bigger than the so-called 'Big Tree' at Victoria Falls. To the Stutchbury clan, it became known as 'The Family Tree'. We all have one of Wayne's paintings of this venerable giant, each depicting a different mood. This arid strip of land is home to the mopane squirrel, impala, baboon and elephant

in transit between the *jesse* and the river. As we progress towards the airstrip, there is another soil change and red sand becomes the order of the day, which is ideal for what is referred to as *jesse* bush, actually a local name for thicket. What few black rhino remain, hide up in the *jesse* and only venture out to water at night, for fear of being killed by poachers. The breeding herds of elephant also favour the *jesse* so it is not an area we use a great deal. Poor visibility, even at the driest time of the year, and tangled undergrowth, comprising not only small scrub, but also great patches of *Acacia ataxacantha* and *Acacia schweinfurthii,* does not make it the ideal viewing habitat. I do love the sound of the name *Acacia schweinfurthii* — it is so apt as it grabs you every which way.

Neighbours with guns

Being adjacent to a hunting area we do, on occasions, hear the shots as the hunters pursue their trophies. Unfortunately, hunters' shots are not the only ones we hear. Poaching has been very heavy and concentrated in the valley and since 1984, when a special task force called 'Operation Stronghold' was set up by National Parks, we have often become involved in anti-poaching exercises. This is mainly because of our location, but also because we wanted to help. Help given in the form of resupplies of food and drink and the chance of a shower for the men on active follow-ups or even routine patrols. Often too, our radio works when theirs does not, so we assist with communications and transport to Kariba if necessary.

We did get extremely involved in one particular exercise

Black rhinoceros generally keep to thickly wooded areas rather than open grasslands, but Suzie did not conform and spent many hours on the open floodplain. Suzie's horn formation was unusual in that the back horn was far longer than the front horn. The combined weight of the two horns would have been irresistible to poachers.

Right: Suzie's long back horn, seen here in silhouette against the Zambian escarpment, illustrates her vulnerability as she persisted feeding on the floodplain in broad daylight in full view of the Zambian bank.

in 1986. The bulk of the action was at Chewore, which is approximately eighty kilometres downstream. One of the men had twisted his ankle very badly so he was brought back to camp whilst the other rangers continued to track. They lost the tracks during the night and the poachers escaped back to Zambia in their dugout canoe, which had been sunk and stashed in a heavy reed bed. All the men were exhausted as it had been a long, arduous, but fruitless exercise. The aircraft came to collect the 'walking wounded' and I took him up to the airstrip. There is a cardinal rule when dealing with unmanned airstrips and that is 'never leave until the aircraft is safely airborne'. I broke the rule. The pilot had given the thumbs-up signal and, as it was dusk and I was supposed to be doing issues at camp, I left them still on the ground. It transpired that, due to a faulty battery they needed to 'swing start'. The magneto switch was on, so once the engine started the aircraft proceeded down the runway without the benefit of a pilot! Because of his injury, the passenger was unable to effectively use the brake pedal, but his half-hearted efforts did get it off the runway and straight into the *jesse* — one way of stopping an aircraft permanently — as the wings snapped off!

From brown to green

Africa is a brown continent and the Zambezi Valley, although it has a major perennial river flowing through it, is a very tawny area except for a few months during the rainy season. At this time the green bursts forth strong and exuberant.

At Chikwenya we are blessed with some truly magnificent evergreen trees, *Trichelia emetica*, Natal mahogany, under which the camp is built. Even within the immediate camp area there are so many different types of trees that a visiting botanist never progressed beyond the camp itself and still not everything was classified. This gives an indication of the diversity of the area, which directly relates to the varying soil types.

Another prominent and unusual tree is the *Kigelia africana*, the sausage tree, named for its long, cylindrical-shaped fruit. Every year we have a competition to see who can find the heaviest sausage still intact and unspoiled. It is not unusual to find fruits weighing in at between seven and nine kilograms. It is not an evergreen tree and drops its leaves in August, prior to blossoming. The leaves are large and brittle making a carpet underneath the tree. However, this carpet does not deaden noise, but accentuates it and actively creates sounds. Normally game passes through the camp in utter silence, particularly elephant. The very soft and squishy pads, which form the base of elephants' feet, allow them to approach without any warning and their enormous weight is displaced over the large area of their pads hardly making a depression even in the soft sand. However, even elephant make crackling noises when walking over this bed of leaves, giving notice of their approach.

The kigelia remain bare for only a short time and the new leaves have an intensity of colour that exceeds that of all the other trees when they first come into leaf. Pure leaf green forms a perfect foil for the chandeliers of burgundy-coloured blooms which festoon the bare branches just before the appearance of the leaves. Kigelia blossoms have an incredibly lustrous look and always make me want to stroke them. There is an apparently velvety texture to these huge blooms, which often do not have time to develop fully before they are devoured with great enthusiasm by the vervet monkey, baboon, impala and bushbuck. Vervet monkey also treat themselves to a 'champagne breakfast' when they sit sipping the nectar from the cup of the bloom before actually eating it. During the night we often have a fitful breeze and find, in the early morning, that there is a burgundy overlay on the straw coloured carpet of leaves. This does not last long as the blossoms are considered to be such a delicacy by the game and Mattias, our chef, is hard pressed to find even one flower for his lunchtime display on the buffet table. The remains of the chandeliers hang bare for a short while and then, one day, we notice that the trees are covered with young sausages. These are bright green too, and at this early stage, still soft, pliable and palatable.

Wild animals often provide comic opera views of themselves, probably because we tend to elevate them above their real station in life. For instance, the kudu is usually seen as a regal antelope, but when hungry and seeking a change of diet, a mature kudu bull with a half formed sausage sticking out of his mouth on either side, looks quite silly.

Once the fruit is fully formed and dry it is not generally favoured by the game, but in its young form it is eaten by

Elephant often feed on young sausages — the fruit of the Kigelia africana — so preventing them filling out and maturing. Other species enjoy the sausages too and there is possibly some sort of natural control at work here. Kigelias usually show an elephant browse line-high.

kudu, bushbuck, baboon and elephant. Rhinoceros seem to be the only user of the kigelia fruit when it is fully mature and certainly, in our area, you can guarantee that you will find some young kigelia trees adjacent to well-established rhino middens.

Because the kigelia is one of the first trees to get a full canopy of leaves in summer, we find it is often favoured by leopard as an ideal place to store a half-eaten carcase. The leaves not only keep the meat cool, but also prevent vulture from seeing the carcase and descending onto the remains. Being able to secure one's next meal in a tree high enough to prevent the earthbound hyena and jackal appropriating it, is an advantage for the leopard, and except in very rare cases, adult lion cannot easily climb the steep trunks of these 'larder' trees. Generally the leopard can rely on having secured meals for two or three days, depending on the size of the prey. The other trees which leopard often use are the *Trichelia emetica*, Natal mahogany, and as these are virtually evergreen, they fulfil the same function of preventing the crime of carcase stealing by the ever vigilant vulture.

In camp we have tried, within reasonable limits, to remove as little of the vegetation as possible. Of course, during the rains, we do have to cut short the grass which grows high enough to hide an elephant. We also have to clear some sort of a pathway from the huts to the dining area and allow for sufficient visibility at night for safe progress to and from these areas. We have a continuing battle with the thicket, which constantly encroaches. But it does provide 'walls' for the dining room when it climbs to join the canopy.

33

Elephant *al fresco*

One afternoon in camp, Sapi, an elephant bull who was 'resident', caused a good deal of embarrassment to me in the dining area. Everyone had gone out on the drives after tea, or so I thought, when Sapi approached the wall of creepers. He proceeded to tear down, with dedication, great chunks of vegetation. I approached to what I considered to be safe range and then tried to stop him from destroying our 'dining room' entirely by clapping hands and making a big noise and shouting at him to, 'Stop it!' Unknown to me, there were a couple of guests who had stayed behind and they were more than amused to watch this pantomime. Sapi initially appeared to take heed and stopped feeding. He looked around at me in a guilty manner, but once he was confident that I had disappeared, continued with increased enthusiasm to pull the place apart. The observers swore that he knew what was going on, as he kept looking backwards to check if I was returning and apparently, literally stuffed his mouth with all the luscious goodies that he had pulled down and then moved off rather quickly as if to escape from the scene of the crime.

The combretum is one of the largest flora families and we have at least six different combretums in camp. The large *Combretum imberbe*, leadwood, is easy to distinguish with its definite bark pattern, small leaves and seed pods. Leadwood is one of the most incredibly hard woods we have encountered. It is so hard that even the powerful termites cannot destroy it and so we try to use it, where possible, in building. It is extremely difficult to work with and over the years we must have broken hundreds, if not thousands, of axe heads and saw blades on the leadwoods.

We never cut a living tree for firewood, but we are permitted to collect the timbers which have been pushed down by elephant, and only ever bother to collect leadwood and mopane. Acacias go up in a puff of smoke and some of the other trees have a pungent smell when burnt, which sometimes taints food. When the campfire dies down and the flames are subdued so that only a glow remains, it can clearly be seen from the embers which wood is which. The leadwood burns very slowly, the wood is finely grained and the definition of the bark remains intact even when the log is burnt. The ash which remains is almost pure white. The mopane, which also

Bush chandeliers. The blossoms of the Kigelia africana develop over a period of time from the top downwards and sometimes we see small green fruits forming at the top of the chandeliers, while flowers are still opening at the bottom of the arrangement.

Right: The epitome of feline grace. This hard-to-see leopard allowed himself to be photographed before disappearing unhurriedly into the deepening dusk. The stance is typical, head down and tail curved, showing the white underparts - a common feature in the animal world. Its dual purpose is to act as a follow-me sign for the young and as an alarm signal.

The exception rather than the rule. The 'larder' tree is an Acacia albida. A large proportion of leopard kills are male impala. It seems that the rams are less alert, and the horns help to lodge the kill in the tree.

burns slowly, disintegrates more easily and does not retain its form. The camp fireplace is the heart of any camp. Ours is placed near the edge of the river terrace and, unobscured by any vegetation, provides a clear view across the sandy river bed and the floodplain — magical and mystical on moonlit nights. It has been a gathering place from primeval times offering safety, warmth and companionship. It is a place to talk and a place to listen.

The dining area is not roofed. The 'ceiling' consists of mahogany and albida leaves and the 'walls' are combretum

The camp is open and unfenced. No restrictions are ever imposed on the natural inhabitants of the area and no damage is done by them to any of the buildings. A commonly held belief was that the elephants would eat the thatch, but this has not happened, even though thatch could be classed as part of their normal diet, as it is simply dry grass.

creepers, interspersed with *lianes*, vines, such as *Artabotrys brachypettalus* or *Cocculus hirsutis* and *Combretum microphyllum/paniculatum,* the flame combretum. What a collection of tongue twisters! The latter is a climbing combretum and provides a violent splash of scarlet like an umbrella in the springtime. During most of the year it is just another series of vines, graceful certainly, but in September it comes into its own and takes the throne for a short while. It is at that time when the birds, especially the sunbirds, revel in the sudden increase in the supply of nectar. Blackeyed bulbuls, commonly called toppies, normally have a greyish-beige chest but in springtime they become stained or coloured by the microphyllum. This causes quite a bit of confusion amongst the birdwatchers in camp as they are convinced they have found a new species!

The luncheon buffet layout is designed to encourage guests to eat and enjoy, and with Jeff, as always, eager to taste and test. Everybody enjoys meals al fresco, including the elephant.

Always evergreen, the Natal mahoganies provide a shady, cool area under which the guests relax, eat, swap stories and compare notes of what has been seen and photographed.

Caution — wild animals

In the valley there is a very coarse, tall grass which grows in clumps and which can reach heights of more than three metres. It is often called elephant grass. The correct botanical name is *Vetevaria* but at Chikwenya we call it 'adrenalin' grass. It tends to grow in low-lying areas such as the bottom of river gulleys and in *vleis*, marshy areas, on clay based soils. The game do not really favour it, presumably because it is too coarse, but after the more succulent annual grasses have been eaten or have died back, the hungry animals have no option but to eat it, if only for fodder and bulk. It is so thick, strong, high and dense in places that even the Land Rovers battle to get through and, if you venture into the *Vetevaria* on foot, you will soon appreciate why we call it adrenalin grass. So many rustles and obscure menacing sounds seem to emanate from the middle of a patch of this grass, that even if it is not providing cover for a herd of elephant, a pride of lion or an irritable old buffalo, one still feels a definite sense of unease. I suppose this is because we humans cannot rely on our senses of smell or hearing to a high degree and therefore, when our vision is limited, we feel insecure.

Given that predators can disappear behind three or four blades of grass, even while we are watching, I believe that the degree of caution we employ before venturing into the adrenalin grass is fully justified. Towards the end of the dry season, this vegetation is bleached to an old gold colour and provides an ideal camouflage for tawny gold and grey lion. Some of the clumps of *Vetevaria* are regularly fed upon by the elephant from the beginning of the season when they are green and presumably more palatable. This constant topping encourages new growth so the patches of green adrenalin grass

lack impact as they are short and more open. From the camp we look straight over the Zambezi River to Chikwenya Island. It is one of the largest islands to be found on this stretch of the river. Six kilometres long and at least two kilometres wide, it provides us with a buffer against development on the Zambian side of the river. Beyond the island, which is well-wooded with evergreen trichelia at the western end, one sees the Zambian escarpment on the horizon. This a good looking range of hills and provides the frame of our amphitheatre.

Each year the Zambian hills burn. Sometimes this happens from March, when we arrive, through to the end of November, when we leave. The fires are often spectacular, and although we deplore the continual destruction that results from these slow burns, we cannot help but gasp at the spectacular effects it creates. Flames reaching high into the sky from the summits of the escarpment are boldly reflected and enlarged in the smooth waters of the Zambezi. Insects and smaller reptiles are undoubtedly consumed by the flames, but the bigger mammals escape and benefit from the lush new growth.

Girl, the young lioness, boldly staring, but in relaxed stance, in the adrenalin grass, illustrating yet again the marvels of camouflage. Positively identifying lionesses is never easy, as one actually has to learn to recognise the whisker spots, but Girl gave us some help as she had a beauty spot between her whiskers.

38

High powered sustenance

Elephant continuously spread and redistribute many species of trees and plants through the entire range of their chosen habitat. We have noticed this particularly on the eastern end of Chikwenya Island, where over the past seven years, there has been a marked increase in the number of young albida trees which are now well established and forming a woodland. This disproves the theory that the albida cannot regenerate without having an annual overlay of alluvial soil as top dressing. Chikwenya Island was originally a sandbar which developed into an area of open grassland with a few clumps of *Phragmites* in sheltered bays and pools. The elephant have embarked on a massive, natural, replanting exercise by virtue of their frequent visits to this island, where their dollops of steaming dung, full of fresh albida seeds, have effectively formed a built-in compost, encouraging good germination. This concentration of one variety of tree is in this case an asset, as the albida is such a rich source of nourishment to all the game, providing thirty five to forty per cent of protein per ton.

The backwaters of the channel provide ideal growing conditions for the *Eichhornia crassites*, water hyacinth, yet another exotic aquatic plant which has established itself in Zimbabwean waters. In March, when we come around the corner into the channel, we see a field of pale, delicate, mauve hyacinths. Flowers and leaves alike are entire and unspoiled at this time of year as there is no need for the game to feed off them when there is such an abundance of grass. They resemble iris blossoms and personally I feel that they do not belong in the valley, but should be growing in more formal conditions. Their particular colour is not natural for Africa. It seems too soft and muted. Notwithstanding the fact that it is not indigenous, and my feeling that it does not belong, the flowers in particular are relished by the herds of buffalo and towards the end of the dry season they seem to enjoy the leaves as well. I doubt that there is much food value in them as they are so airy, but the fields get cropped low in October of each year and regrow even more vigorously during the rains, presenting a sight that is reminiscent of the fields of flowers cultivated in Holland.

Foodstuffs with a high protein content, such as apple-ring pods are preferred to dry, bulk fodder, although variety is essential to the diet. Big John feeds high on the Acacia albida, lowering his hindquarters in preparation for the ultimate effort of standing on his two back legs to reach the limit.

Water lilies are indigenous and are fed on by baboon who eat not only the flower heads but also the bulbs. The flowers provide an enormous amount of nectar for the bees in the valley, who produce a delicious wild honey.

Left: *Unappealing to look at, the scraggly growth of the Caparris tomentosa more than justifies its existence with the appearance of its delicate, richly-scented flowers. It is a vigorous climber, very often overtaking and killing the tree it uses for support.*

Above left: *The regeneration of numerous species of plants and trees is assisted when the seeds pass through the digestive system of wild animals. Elephant are largely responsible for the successful regeneration of Acacia albida on Chikwenya Island. Dung beetles also assist in breaking up the fibres and spreading the seeds.*

Chanel No 5

A number of the riverine trees seem to be very heavily scented and, although they occur in an intermittent growth pattern, they tend to overpower less strong but more subtle smells. We are always aware of the mahogany blooms, as the fragrance wafts through the camp, but the intensity of their perfume is rivalled by the scent of the *Caparris tomentosa*, a spiny and not very attractive creeping bush, but with beautiful, delicate, white flowers whose droopy tendrils are tipped with maroon. Wild flowers never last for a long time, but one takes over from another, and so when the mahogany and caparris have spent their force, the very pervasive scent of the *Diospyros senencis* is noticed.

The faces are easily visible on each bloom of the spray of water hyacinth, still intact at the beginning of the season. Later in the year the buffalo will have eaten them.

Fields of mauve water hyacinth give a surrealistic impression as we explore the river on the first cruise of the season. Sapi, accompanied by the ubiquitous cattle egrets, is beginning to crop this field of blossoms, introducing some variety to his diet.

Puncture material

The diospyros is our 'worst' tree. Everybody who has ever driven a vehicle in the valley will agree that the penetrating powers of the thorny spines of the diospyros equal, if not exceed, those of a huge nail. Other thorns may look more spectacular and hazardous, such as the 'Y' shaped sharp thorns of the *Balanites maughamii* or the wicked looking spines of the *Maclura africana* which the elephant discard all over the 'road', but I am truly convinced that diospyros are the real villains and they are always referred to as 'puncture material'. The tree itself is not particularly attractive but all is forgiven when it comes into bloom, well after the others, spreading its own signal that the rains are not too far off. The perfume from this tree is strong, dominant and sometimes overpowering. Then there are other blooms, such as the star-shaped, white flowers of the *Byrsocarpus orientalis*, which have such a delicate scent that one doubts one's nose. It is such a great pity that their exquisite display lasts for only one day.

I find that one of the most difficult things to describe well is a smell, but everyone will recognize the scent of the 'baked-potato plant', as this is easy to associate with and relate to. The plant is so irritatingly inconspicuous that it is difficult to pinpoint where that delicious mouth-watering smell is coming from. It is a small shrub called *Phyllanthus reticulata,* whose tiny, tight, white florets give out that smell which we associate with the return to camp at the end of the day.

Wide open spaces

To the east of the camp we have a magical mixed albida woodland which becomes a fairytale park after the first rains. This comes to an end on the edge of an old river terrace which then gives way to a huge, dry, grassy plain, dotted with an occasional lone albida, and then once more the river. It is here that the vast, open grasslands, bleached to a light blond, march towards the horizon, where, in stark majesty the peaks of the escarpment tower to the skies. The grandeur and spectacle of the mountain vistas defy description, but what always impresses me most is the range of their colours which encompasses the entire spectrum. Sometimes they are burnt orange, sometimes muted grey, often plain ordinary brown, and occasionally bright green, but mostly violet, smoke blue

The geological explanation for the red cliffs is obviously that the colour is mineral-based. The bee-eaters use cliffs for their breeding tunnels and these whitefronted bee-eaters have moved away from the crumbling river bank into the firmer sandstone of the red cliffs.

and purple in the early morning or late evening light, never constant, but always majestic.

Downstream, the river takes a wide curve and far to the east we see the Chewore range of hills, with the more regulated growth pattern of mopane woodlands in the mid-distance.

Behind the camp, towards the airstrip, the Sapi River bends to present us with yet another awesome landscape. Huge, steep, stark, orangey-red sandstone cliffs occur on one side of the dry river bed, providing a strong contrast to the white river sand at their base. These cliffs erode when the river rushes down in flood and when we re-explore the area at the beginning of each season, we come across enormous, sometimes totally intact, sheets of red cliff which have, apparently, just gently dropped off the face of the high cliffs. What a sight it would be to see the dirty, swollen river in full flood being attacked by large slices of flying cliff face.

Opposite the red cliffs is yet another different vegetation zone. This time we have open grasslands, but not *Vetevaria,* in patches interspersed with clumps of *Lonchocarpus capassa* , rain trees, and the vivid, orangey-yellow flowering *Cassia abbreviata.* Gradually the soil changes and we enter an acid zone which encourages the growth of the *Hypheane benguellensis,* northern ilala palms, as well as increased numbers of baobabs, mopane and *Garcinia Livingstonia,* African mangosteen. In Botswana this tree thrives right in the middle of the Okavango Delta, with its feet almost always wet, but in the Zambezi Valley it seems confined to the edge of the mopane veld. I wonder why? There is so much still to learn, but what a wonderful classroom we have.

Our great trek

The annual migration

Our lives are controlled by the seasons and each year we undertake our own migration in and out of the valley. For us, March is a time of expectancy. We are excited and enthusiastic, having been away from the valley for three months. We have recharged our personal batteries, as well as having reconditioned all the vehicles and machinery. Spirits are high as we set off from Kariba. The distance from Kariba to Chikwenya is just over two hundred kilometres, some of it on tarred roads, but the bulk of the journey is over gravel and bush tracks. We usually form a ragbag convoy with the company vehicles and our own Land Rover. All are loaded to the hilt with us, our staff, our provisions for the next few weeks and an assortment of items which we consider essential to the eventual completion of the journey. Two hundred kilometres is not far, but we allow a full day to reach camp and also make provision for having to sleep on the road. We carry the basics in terms of bedding, as well as a good supply of water and foodstuffs.

Pioneering

We know that we are bound to have some problems *en route* as some of the roads have not been used at all since we left camp at the end of the previous dry season. During the rainy season the National Parks staff use either aircraft or boats to move about the valley and we are the first people to use the roads. Annual road work and maintenance does not take place until May when everything is really dry again. For this reason, we set off armed with an assortment of shovels, axes, picks, cane knives, as well as coils of ropes, chains and cables, which will be used to tow vehicles in or out of muddy river beds or swampy, sticky patches. These sticky patches cannot be avoided. Often it seems that the original road makers deliberately ran the road straight through the 'pans' which fill during the rains and hold water until mid-August. Pans occur in low-lying patches of land, where a small amount of water initially collects. They are utilized by game and, over a period of time, the movement of the game, combined with the effects of their wallowing and rolling in the mud, make well-puddled depressions. The pans provide inland water for the wild

Very different vistas greet us on our return. The path to the house is barely perceptible after a good rainy season. By July, the ground is bare again, but for this year, at least, there will be food for all. In March and April, the albidas are almost bare, with grey leaves dropping in preparation for their winter flush.

animals, thereby ensuring that they are more evenly distributed throughout the valley.

When we first went to to Chikwenya, the country was experiencing a series of droughts and the annual rainfall figures fell to less than half the normal average. On these initial trips into camp therefore, we only had to keep the vehicles going. At that time road conditions were not much of a hazard. However, subsequent years have provided more of a challenge. Our rains have lasted well into the month of March and the dirt roads then become muddy, sticky tracks, barely discernible due to the growth and often blocked by trees which have been pushed down by elephant or fallen down through age. Sufficient fresh food to last for at least two weeks while we prepare the camp for guests, in addition to survival type fare such as bully beef and baked beans, is carried with us. Once the drought broke the first return journey

Depending on the pattern of the annual rains, we sometimes see the Sapi, a seasonal river, come down in a flood before we leave camp in November / December. If it still holds water in March, we are guaranteed a tough trip back to camp. Soft, fluffy, cotton-wool clouds are reflected in the estuary, but they soon disappear as winter approaches.

to camp provided us with all sorts of different hazards. Jeff had to remain in town under strict doctor's orders recovering from hepatitis. Wayne, our youngest son, accompanied me on this trip. His not inconsiderable strength, as well as his very definite if somewhat warped sense of humour, were much appreciated. The journey was proceeding according to plan. It seemed as if we would make it in one day, despite the wet weather — until we reached the Sapi River.

Approaching the river crossing, the land rises before giving way to a steep decline to the waters' edge. Normally we see a large expanse of dry, white sand dotted here and there with dollops of elephant dung. On this occasion the astonishing sight that greeted us was an unbroken stretch of two hundred metres of brown, swirling water. We had experienced three years of drought when the Sapi had been a mere trickle. This time it was a strong, fast flowing river forming an effective barrier against any immediate further progress. All vehicles lurched and skidded to a halt. Everyone debussed, slithered and slid their way down to the river and stared in amazement. This water hazard was an unusual challenge and we hoped that our stock of spark plugs would prove adequate.

A living dipstick

Having a not inconsiderable length of leg, it is usually my task to assess the depth of any unknown stretch of water. I plunged in, and after a few steps, the water reached to my waist. I had trouble keeping my footing. We were not going anywhere in a hurry that day!

The nature of these annual rivers is such that they come down in flood very quickly, but they cease to run equally quickly. We had no way of even guessing how much rain was falling in the catchment area, but realised that two metres of water would take some time to dissipate.

Immediate relief was got from making tea. For us it is the panacea for all ills. We then set about planning the route we would take once the river had dropped. The men started collecting firewood and cut branches which we would lay as a 'corduroy' across the muddy, recently flooded areas, to prevent the vehicles sinking. Having done this, a feeling of lassitude developed. To avoid this becoming permanent, we all indulged in energetic water games. We also blew up a spare tube from the Land Rover and taking turns, used it to float gently down the still swollen river. Wayne volunteered to go all the way to camp on the tube and couldn't understand why I rejected this particular plan with some degree of asperity.

Unwelcome attentions

Preparations were made for more tea and a scratch meal. We knew by now that we would have to spend the night by the river, so we started trying to smooth out the ground and organise ourselves for sleep. For some totally unknown reason, I elected to sleep in the front of the Land Rover. Why I ever thought I could sleep with the gear stick and the steering wheel poking whichever part of my body presented itself, I'll never know. My head hung over the edge of the seat and out of one door, while my legs hung out of the other door. Wayne didn't fare much better. He was on the wet ground, using as a pillow, a package containing new staff uniforms wrapped in slippery plastic that crackled and slid every time he moved. The rest of the staff were scattered around the other vehicles, some on the ground and some on the seats, all draped with mosquito nets. As there was nothing suitable to hang them from and as we did not have the rings with us, they clung to our unprotected limbs and offered no protection from the millions of starving mosquitoes.

It was not a good night, but early dawn showed only the remnants of the flood waters. Everyone thought that we would soon be across the Sapi River as half a metre of water is not a problem to a Land Rover. While the men laid the branches and logs down, I too decided to use the time constructively. I put down my grubby bit of canvas in the middle of a relatively clear and dry bit of ground, and proceeded to cut my toenails and pluck my eyebrows. Thinking back on it I must have presented a most incongruous sight. I was clad in a swimsuit at the time and engaged in feminine tasks which normally take place, if not in a beauty parlour, at least in the privacy of one's own bedroom!

The last leg

Finally we succeeded, got all the vehicles across and were then on the home stretch with only fifteen kilometres to camp, but fate worked against us again. Each vehicle got stuck, right down to the axles stuck, in a *vlei,* marshy ground, just three kilometres from home. We abandoned the vehicles and walked to camp with the most important pieces of equipment carried either conventionally, in our hands, or traditionally, on our heads. A proper safari in fact; Doctor Livingstone would surely have approved.

The mopane woodland, which links the main access road and our camp road, is in full, fresh leaf as we drive through on our way into camp for the new season. Once we break out of the mopane, we are into the jesse and on the last leg of our journey.

After two days of sunshine we recovered the Land Rovers, deciding at the same time to cut a new access road into camp, avoiding the low-lying marshy areas. At this stage I should give an explanation of our interpretation of the word, 'road'. It should be called, 'track' and in essence it is any ground along which one can drive a Land Rover with relative ease and only moderate discomfort. It also means an area from which only the 'impossible to avoid' trees have been cut, leaving anything around which we can drive, still standing.

An extended journey

Not wanting to labour the point, I feel I must recount the tale of our most extended journey into the interior. Again we had late rains and became impatient as we sat in Kariba waiting for what could be considered suitable weather. Desperation and impatience won the day and ignoring all advice we set off in excessively wet conditions, having made more than usually thorough preparations for sleeping and and eating *en route*.

Despite these plans, or perhaps because of them, we took four days to cover a distance which, when the roads are in good order, takes four hours. There are a number of small streams and *spruits* on the road which are normally easy to negotiate. The real 'baddies' as far as rivers go, are usually the big sandy rivers like the Chiruwe and the Sapi. We were anticipating trouble getting across them as we knew, in advance, that they were full and flowing. What we did not know in advance, was that the volume of water which had poured down from the escarpment was so enormous. The normally dry, little river courses, usually quite insignificant and certainly not a hazard, were raging torrents of flood waters. When the waters slowed down, they left behind a three metre-high perpendicular bank. All the approaches had been washed away.

This time the formula was to get out and grab your shovel, spade or pick, and move the soil sufficiently to allow the Land Rovers to drive down the steep slope without toppling over. The next step was to cover the really muddy patches at the bottom of the river bed with logs and branches and then dig the opposite bank down to a gradient which was feasible and safe for the vehicles and us. Of course we got stuck. Many times we towed each other out. Frequently we got water in the electrics of the vehicles. We were consistently covered in mud, and we were hot, tired, thirsty, fed up, irritable and hungry, but determined. We made it, much to the surprise of the National Parks staff who had said the road was impassable.

It took us four days of hard slog, relieved by little incidents which sometimes developed into full scale comic opera. We had with us a driver, newly qualified, who had not driven in such conditions before. The general rule is to engage second gear, four wheel drive, and keep your revs up. The sight of Jeff in his newly painted Land Rover becoming airborne for at least twenty metres, having hit a solid lump in the midst of one of these fast attacks, must have made our new employee wish he had not learnt to drive. I was very thankful that the suspension had just been overhauled.

The four day endurance test that we had to undergo one year, provided a bonus for the hyena en route. Hyena seem to be addicted to ditches and culverts, where they enjoy plopping themselves into the muddy water.

Survival fare

Our fresh supplies are carried with us, carefully packed in cooler boxes and covered with blankets and tarpaulins to keep off the worst of the heat. However, cooler boxes were not designed to keep perishable food in good condition over a four day period and our fresh food did not survive the rigours of that journey. The sweet smell of putrefying flesh greeted me each time I opened the back door of the Land Rover.

While I am not a vegetarian I can easily survive without meat and I discarded the assorted and overmature joints without too many qualms. Hyenas *en route* must have been delighted with the unexpected feasts we provided for them and we broke out the 'hard tack'. Jeff loves baked beans and hates bully beef. Glenn, our second son loves bully beef and hates baked beans and I am not crazy about either dish. The continuous rains ensured there was no way to organize a resupply so we had little choice — bully and beans or beans and bully. Although we always bring in fishing worms, there is usually no time to fish and on this occasion the worms had drowned! The first guests were more than welcome that season, not just for themselves but also for the fresh foods arriving on the aircraft with them! In fact we all went up to the airstrip to greet them and gloat over the resupply.

Typically the sunsets at the beginning of the season are clear and strong, with outlines of vegetation and landscape not yet softened by the smoke haze, which will develop later in the year. One of the joys of living on the river is the variety of skies. We never see the same picture twice.

The march of the seasons

Upside down moon

Being away from the artificial conditions imposed by urban living means that are our lives are influenced and even controlled by the seasons. When you operate a safari camp you have two sets of seasons; the camp season and the natural season. In most parts of the world the seasons match. Spring, summer and autumn are logical and clearly defined holiday times. This is not so in Zimbabwe. Our camp is either busy or closed; it is busy during the dry months and closed for the rainy season. The natural seasons are basically either wet or dry and there is far more dry than wet.

In the southern hemisphere everything is turned about for those visitors who have spent all their lives in the north. The night skies are truly brilliant but unfamiliar and have to be explained. The new moon is upside down and where we live the belief is that it is placed that way to ensure that it can catch and store any rain which may fall, water being so very precious to us. It is not only the stars that confuse visitors. The seasons too, are in reverse and also ill defined. Because of our latitude of 17°S we do not have extremes in the length of

our days. Our longest day falls on 21 December when sunset occurs at about quarter to seven while at the other end of the scale the shortest mid-winter day is on 21 June and then we lose the sun at quarter to six so there is just one hour's difference.

Logically one must start at the beginning of the Chikwenya season, March, when we return to re-open the camp and this is always an experience.

The hammerkop is a fishing bird best known for the enormous nest he constructs out of twigs, branches and bits of bone. There is a nest in one of the big trees adjacent to this annual pan and so it has become known as Hammerkop Pool. In the early months of the year, we find evidence of frenzied nesting activities in the form of weavers' colonies. Weavers always build close to water and favour thorn trees if possible, as these trees give a measure of protection against predators, such as snakes and leguaans.

Our albida woodland in late November looks, for all the world, like a carefully kept park. Fresh, green grass has sprung up after the first rains. This is what we left behind, and as we return, we cannot help wondering what we will find.

What will we find?

We never know what has transpired in the three months that we have been away and after doing battle with non-existent roads, blocked by trees pushed over by elephant, and river crossings eroded beyond recognition, we find that the anticipation builds up as we get nearer the big baobab and the camp.

Are the buildings still going to be intact or have the white ants finally won the never-ending battle? Has the Zambezi River changed its course dramatically and left us with nowhere to launch the boats or pump water? All these thoughts go through our minds as we drive through the last few kilometres of thicket known as *jesse*. Each year we are fortunate to spend many hours observing and to some extent 'getting to know' the resident animals in our immediate vicinity. Some inevitably move off or die, but others move in and then we observe how the newcomers establish themselves in the ever-changing scene at Chikwenya.

We expect the rainy season, which usually commences in November, to begin to tail off in March and finish in April. That is how it should be in normal years, but in common with the rest of the world our weather pattern does seem to be changing and the rainy season is tending to both start and end later. We hope that enough rain has fallen to encourage good growth which will ensure survival and successful raising of the young of all the species. From April, dry weather should prevail until November when the clouds will once again begin to form and fill with moisture, signalling the start of the annual rains.

The camp is totally different at either end of the season. In March it is green, vibrant and lush. Visibility is almost nil

Opposite: The natural flow and the annual floods of the Zambezi River have been curtailed by Kariba Dam. There is now a rise and fall in the level of the river caused by the variations of the hydro-electric projects at Kariba and Kafue. This has caused a marked increase in bank erosion and each year we lose many trees to the river. However, the albidas have a very long tap root and often remain anchored to the bank. Weaver birds — usually spottedbacked — are the first to take advantage of the branches hanging over water, as safe sites for their nests. Again the destruction of one form of life assists in the creation of another.

A variety of colours and forms develop each year — some water lilies bloom early in the season, some later and some not at all. The pattern of rainfall dictates the timing and this also applies to the growth of annuals.

Below: *Pans full of water lilies break up the woodland terraces, which lie to the east of the camp. Sadly, neither the pans nor the water lilies last long, as the season becomes progressively drier.*

when we drive through the *jesse* and I am always relieved that we do not meet the breeding herds of elephant on the road as we may not be able to avoid a collision. The grass is high and the pans are full of water and seasonal water lilies. Trees are festooned with weavers' nests and the air is alive with the chirruping of insects, as well as the chirping of birds and chicks. The 'nasties' too, are plentiful — snakes and scorpions and centipedes and spiders all thrive in the hot, moist conditions undisturbed by our habitual cleaning and sweeping. Everything is full and fresh and fascinating, partly because we have missed being in the bush and in constant touch with the natural world, and partly because it is that time of the year. The rains have been good and given new life for another year and we gloat about the amount of rain which has fallen as this provides abundant grazing for the herds. This was especially true of the years immediately following the drought years. We had become accustomed to seeing hundreds of starving animals, trying to find enough food just to keep alive for one more day. The gaunt and haggard faces of the impala were truly pitiful; equally pathetic were the starving elephant and hippo which are normally such rounded creatures. The skeletal appearance of these species in drought years seems to have more than normal impact and causes us great distress. We now rejoice that the place is green and the flanks are round and all is well. The quality of light too is most special at this time of the year. It is luminescent due, I suppose, to the perfectly clean air. The smoke haze has been washed away and there is such an intensity and purity of light that the folds and tucks in the skirt of the Zambian escarpment appear to be viewed through rose-tinted and three-dimensional glasses.

The young impala have now got to the leggy stage, but

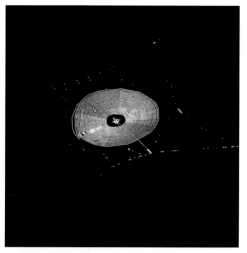

numbers of new, fluffy, chocolate brown buffalo calves suddenly seem to appear and very occasionally they break out with a hop and a skip and a jump. Buffalo calves take life seriously and never seem to frolic as do most other infants and young — what can be the reason? We delight in becoming reacquainted with the resident game and having, yet again, the hugeness of the valley available at all times. For us, no more tightly drawn curtains or locked doors, and instead, what some people consider to be miles and miles of 'bloody' Africa. Although there is a constancy and strong sense of continuity in the bush, there are also annual changes wrought by the power of the elements. The ever-changing course of the river has to be plotted in Jeff's mind, but this cannot be done until the camp itself is in reasonable working order. Every year the immediate outlook from our house and the dining area across the floodplain has to be reviewed.

Left: *This nursery herd of impala lambs will eventually grow into themselves, but when first born and still new they appear to be all legs and heads. They do seem to be very vulnerable when left alone like this.*

Right: *A welcome and wonderful sight of resident elephant bulls returning to the mainland after feeding on Chikwenya Island. Elephant bulls tend to live outside the breeding herds forming loose associations which may last for an hour, a day or even a week. It is not uncommon to see an elephant bull alone and lone bulls are by no means all 'rogue' bulls.*

Blinkers off

Guests admire our superior vision, but this is simply because we are able to recognize shapes and shadows and also we know the landscape intimately. When a tree falls down, that gap has to slowly imprint itself into our subconscious, until everything fits and again becomes familiar. The dry, sandy river bed of the Sapi needs to be looked at slowly and carefully. New logs of wood have been left high and dry from the flooding. The old, familiar stumps and clumps of grass are no longer where they were. Not only do we have to become accustomed to the new backdrop, but also we have to sharpen our vision. Eyes have grown lazy during the rainy season and focussing binoculars is no longer automatic. We have to practise a little in all spheres and listen hard and long before we can accurately identify the numerous bird calls. The vegetation provides a few hurdles. Not only is it in full flush, but while away we have been looking at highveld trees, so there is a tendency to hesitate a little when asked, 'What tree is that?' But it soon falls into place again now we are home.

Jeff on his beloved Nkwazi gently bumbling upstream at the end of a cruise. Viewing game from the water, both on Lake Kariba and the Zambezi River, gives an added dimension to the safari and this trimaran design, using stable Canadian canoe hulls, has proved to be the ideal craft for shallow river conditions.

Spit and polish

Jeff's first love is his boat, *Nkwazi*, fish eagle. He is always desperate to get it back on the water, but annual maintenance with another layer of fibreglass is essential over the areas which have had contact with stumps or the odd hippo. The decking, too, must have a facelift so we get busy with pots of paint and brushes. There lives in one of my files, a list which gets updated each year and it is called, 'Tasks to do before the guests arrive'. This list is brought out in March. Over the years we have developed a routine and the staff know what to expect. They also know what should be accorded the highest degree of priority. Either *'Nkwazi'* or my office, or both!

Slowly falling temperatures signal the coming of autumn, but the change is imperceptible. As the weather cools down, the tempo of the camp hots up with the increased flow of guests. April and May are special months. The air is crystalline, the escarpment stands proudly in relief and the stars seem to jump out of the sky each night. The game is in prime condition with no evidence of hardship or deprivation and there is a tangible aura of well-being.

June brings us muted shades with almost all the vegetation wearing winter dress. The nights are cold — sometimes four blankets cold — with swirls of river mist gradually burnt off by the rising sun as it gathers strength. The last of the migrant birds have finally flown north; so no more carmines, woodland kingfishers, redwinged pratincoles or swallows. Reptiles are preparing for their annual slow down, in anticipation of which they indulge in a final feeding frenzy. The bush snakes are demolishing the tree frogs at an alarming rate. Hazy conditions prevail as always, due to the inevitable burning in Zambia, but the advantages to the photographer are apparent in the sunsets, which daily seem to get stronger and more dramatic.

Back to front

As if to create even more confusion amongst visitors, our trees reverse the order of colours normally accepted as the natural progression. The deciduous trees do drop their leaves, generally for about three months roughly coinciding with our winter. It is now very dry; we have had no rain for six months and when the temperatures soar, and still the trees come into flush, we wonder just where the moisture is being drawn from. There must be a huge reservoir deep down in the bowels of the earth.

By August the bush is drying up, the viewing is getting better and the weather is getting warmer. We are beginning to see nyala again, as they have to come out of the thicket for water. The carmine bee-eaters are returning, as are the

Winter dress soon creeps in and the lively greens fade. Kudu are now seen more often and readily pose, but their cryptic colours blend and merge so that we do not always spot them. Riverine species such as kudu, bushbuck and nyala have extra large ears, as hearing becomes the most important of the senses when vision is restricted by dense growth.

Promise of rain: a late afternoon build up of heavy and menacing clouds is usual in October, often with no results except for strong winds. But our expectations run high and we wait, hopefully.

skimmers and some of the waders. Kudu and bushbuck are appearing out in the open more frequently because there is no water left in the pans. The blossoms have all faded, the fruits and seeds are forming and fresh green leaves flushing. We start to look to the skies hoping for rain clouds. The concentration of game is noticeable as they congregate on the floodplain and in the woodland to feed on the albida pods. The hazy conditions are now permanent with fantastic purply sunsets. The days are lovely and warm although the nights are still chilly.

Spring for us is heralded by autumn shades and autumn is simply a time when the dead leaves drop off the trees and the weather starts to cool down.

Green again

The first signs of spring are exquisite and there are no words to describe the pureness of the green. It is accentuated by the quality of the light and forms a pleasant contrast to the almost drab albidas whose pods are swelling to provide nutriment for all. Bird life continues to improve and another sign of spring is the return of even more waders. Springtime is my favourite season. Almost overnight the bush is ablaze! The kigelia trees are festooned with burgundy-coloured chandeliers in dramatic contrast to the strong yellow blossoms of the *Cordylia africana*, the wild mango. These fluffy blossoms are infested with longtailed glossy starlings. Spring is of very short duration and some years we seem literally to wake up one day and find that spring has been bypassed and summer has arrived.

Suddenly there is colour on the mopanes. The first tight buds of the new leaves open dark maroon, then turn crimson, red, russet, amber, orange, yellow, lemon, lime and ultimately light bright green. This 'artists' palette' effect is exquisite and to my mind the mix and overlay and blend of what we know as spring colours is very much enhanced by the actual shape of the mopane leaves which simulate butterfly wings, large and small. An amazing thing happens to these leaves — during the cooler mornings and evenings they are fully open and lie flat, but as the sun's rays begin to have a searing effect, the leaves slowly close to an upright position and so they conserve their own moisture by reducing the surface area, which is subject to evaporation and scorching from the intense October heat.

Waiting for rain

In late October or early November it gets hotter and hotter and the atmosphere becomes quite electric as we wait for the first rains. One day the small cottonwool clouds begin to form and soon they become ominous black clouds from which the first big, ploppy drops fall. It is the ultimate relief, but short lived. As if at a signal, the rain stops. The clouds spread at an alarming rate and as we look across the floodplain a few elephant stand in *bas relief* in that peculiarly translucent light that usually presages a really heavy storm. The atmosphere is oppressively still, with no movement anywhere and not a sound to be heard. Even the birds stop singing. Then, in the distance, there is a whooshing murmur which rapidly gains volume. The sky is now an evil-looking greenish-black and the surface of the river becomes ruffled by kittens' paws. These grow into cats' paws. The entire river is in a turmoil. Ominous rumbles of thunder roll down the escarpment and lodge in the valley where they wait for the final signal from the Rain God. The light breeze has disappeared. In its place we have a howling gale which comes at full force across the dry, dusty, parched floodplain bringing with it anything that is not anchored down. Large branches are blown off trees and hurled at us and at least half the sand from the Sapi is now lodged in our ears, eyes, noses and mouths. Still we wait, and as the intensity of the wind decreases, so comes the rain, the lifegiving, cool, fresh rain. A great feeling of elation prevails! Many African-born people have a ritual whereby it is imperative to stand out in the first rain, with faces lifted to the sky, rejoicing. The first stormy effects finally calm down into a gentle, steady rainfall which will soak right into the dehydrated earth and activate our annual cycle of growth.

'Phew,' is the feeling at the end of November. This is partly due to the heat and the usual insanity which affects all of us in the 'people' business, and partly because of the seemingly endless tasks involved in shutting down the camp in time to get away before the rains make our roads impassable. Mixed with the desire to get away is a strong feeling of regret that once again we are leaving our home for the alien regions of the highveld.

We are all looking forward to our break during the closed season. However, as is the way, after a few weeks we will be longing to come back. Always there is something new and wondrous to observe and always the magic is there.

My recollections often merge one with another. Impressions which initially are sharp and vivid, soften and perhaps become jumbled. My words are simply an attempt to describe the glories of the seasons.

The end of the season shows the floodplain almost bare of grass. Zebra, even though they generally feed on coarse grasses, are still avoiding the few remaining dry stalks of Vetevaria. As a species, zebra hold out extremely well and a thin zebra is a rare sight because they have a thick layer of subcutaneous fat from which they draw in times of need.

Overleaf: A beautiful sight and one of Jeff's rare records of a big conglomeration of elephants. In our area this happens infrequently. On this occasion, Saucer, together with one other bull, has joined the cows and calves. The grand dame of Chikwenya, along with her extended family, form this aggregation.

Chikwenya

Pure and simple

Chikwenya Safari Camp is in harmony with its surroundings; it blends with them and does not compete with the wilderness. We take care not to interfere with or damage our environment and we must constantly adapt to our changing landscape and never debase or diminish this amazing resource.

Over the years the landscape has been changed by the forces of nature, but we are unwavering in our efforts not to change it for our selfish, human purposes. Examples of natural change can be seen in the creation of Chikwenya Island less than seventy years ago and in more recent times by the sandbar which developed in front of the camp itself.

When we first visited the camp in 1982, the river flowed immediately in front of the huts. In fact we used to moor the boats in the small gulley near Hut Number 6. Over the years the silt deposited by the floodwaters of the Sapi River created the sandbar which has now developed into a well-grassed plain, providing a wealth of year-round grazing to all the game in the area. Although I personally miss having the water in the immediate vicinity, we are so lucky to gain land rather than lose it to the force of the river.

The Zambezi is blessing Chikwenya with its present flow and it certainly blessed us when it created Chikwenya Island. From our camp, we look over the river channel to Chikwenya Island and this view is always full of interest, as the game swim or wade the water to reach the island. The island itself is gaining in a natural way, as the elephant have helped to recolonise it with albida trees. Certainly nature is at work here, shaping the environment and we must not detract from its efforts.

The view from the dining area. Dry grasslands, the river, Chikwenya Island and finally the mountains, neatly framed by the albida trees in the foreground. Sometimes we see Impala, often elephant, and in this case, the Old Daga Boys.

For me, riverbeds, whether full of water or dry, extend an invitation to explore and the area beyond the albida grove beckons strongly. While enjoying a pre-lunch drink the guests appreciate the pristine scenery, with the added bonus of elephant at ease, feeding in front of the house.

Sharing the wilderness

We are living our dream of sharing our love and interest of the wild with others who want to escape the usual cares of their everyday lives. We have a place for them to 'join' with nature. They may come here from the world of men and enjoy an area, as far as possible untouched and still the domain of the creatures who naturally inhabit the wilderness.

The essence of Chikwenya is its atmosphere of the wild, which is almost tangible. Atmosphere is created by the habitat's appeal to our senses. So many places no longer have the spirit to appeal to our senses as they are constructions without heart. We believe that our simple camp makes an extraordinary appeal to the senses.

The visual impact of the river sunsets is stunning. The afterglow dies slowly as the sun dips below the hills that rim the valley. The richness of that last light is tangible; every blade of grass, for an instant, gains a separate identity and stands on its own, highlighted and perfect. Then, darkness takes over and it all merges again into a field of grass and a forest of trees. Every prismatic colour is reflected back off water so smooth, it seems almost glutinous. There is just the faintest gurgle and burble as the river flows steadily on; through the flatlands, through the gorges, stopping momentarily at Cahora Bassa Dam in Mozambique and then, on again, until it gets lost in the multitude of fingers that form the Zambezi Delta.

Nothing is tarted-up at Chikwenya, though we hope the camp provides basic amenities enough to prevent our guests suffering actual discomfort! We aim to make our visitors feel sufficiently at home to begin to remove their town 'blinkers' and really see the wild environment they have come to experience. Our concern is with looking at the wild and not with presenting a contrived or picturesque overview.

Right: Clouds add dimension to the skyline which has been washed to a pure, sharp blue. A few empty nests of the spottedbacked weavers' colony remain. These will not be used again by the weavers, but other birds, such as cut throat finches, may take advantage of a ready-made home.

Rays of reflected and refracted light give this sunset extra impact, not unlike the colourful effects of a holocaust. This sky is bursting with heat and energy. The afterglow is often more impressive than the sunset.

Baboon playgroup

Many animals live in close proximity to the camp and some are virtually resident. We almost always have baboon around the camp and a troop of baboon provides endless varied entertainment. If we have fun watching, they also have fun. Most especially when they are jumping from the branches of the albida tree, in which our bedroom is built, on to the roof of the bedroom, landing with a loud clatter, and then leaping on to the newly thatched roof of the lounge and bathroom downstairs. This downstairs building has a really steep roof and thus provides the most glorious *pfoopfy* slide imaginable for a troop of bored baboons. Even more rewarding for them, I feel sure, is the instant and extreme reaction they get from me and Jeff. We rush around, shouting with rage and frustration, trying to make enough noise to get them off the thatch as quickly, but also as carefully, as possible, before the entire roof gently follows their bare, pink bottoms on to the ground!

There was a time when one old, big dog baboon was becoming far too familiar and making forays and raids into the vegetable store at the back of the kitchen. On one occasion he even went so far as to steal a tray of eggs from the kitchen, literally behind the cook's back — quick as a flash. This really was the last straw so we took the advice of Phillip, who was then the cook, and made a plan to entice him into the vegetable store and lock him in for a while. Then when he was let out, we planned to mass together and make a huge display of ferocity. Finally the day came when he was trapped in the store and the entire staff gathered with their chosen weapons. The cook was brandishing a frying pan which he kept hitting with a wooden spoon, the object being to try and make as unpleasant a noise as possible so that the baboon would

become too scared to ever stray into the kitchen again. But the plan failed dismally. He was now a very angry baboon and was rushing around the store at great speed, totally demolishing everything which was not securely locked up. When we opened the door in the hope that he would rush off into the far distance, he turned the tables on us and presented such a formidable sight that everyone involved took evasive action and hid behind the nearest door. He was back the next day!

Wayne once returned to school from a holiday at home, leaving in my care an orphan known as Gargantua, being a grossly overfed and misformed cuckoo. He had been a very cold, wet and totally bald fledgling when Wayne had found him in the grass. He seemed a doubtful survivor, but survive he did and grew to grotesque proportions. He was so top heavy that he rivalled Mae West or Raquel Welch (depending on your era) and used to topple over and fall flat on his face. I tried to get him to exercise in a gentle fashion, hoping that he might learn to fly and eventually go away. To achieve this, I would leave him perched on the top rail of one of the verandah chairs, teetering precariously as he battled with the forces of gravity. One day I had left him perched there while I went off on a grasshopper hunt to satisfy his voracious appetite. The resident troop of baboon was passing by on its way down to water and we ignored each other as neither presented any threat to the other. Gargantua was cheeping loudly and impatiently and suddenly, to my horror, I saw an adolescent male baboon make a detour via the open verandah and grab Gargantua in passing and stuff him into his mouth! Nature is not kind and gentle but we had broken the rules, albeit with best of intentions, in our efforts to save the chick.

Humans have been referred to as 'The Naked Ape' and baboons have been called 'Almost Human' by respective authors Desmond Morris and Shirley Strum. Has the thirty year gap between these publications taught us anything? Certainly our behaviour patterns and social structures are similar: with baboons, in general, showing less aggression.

77

Out of the nest

Shortly after that, we did manage to feed up and relocate the very young chick of a chinspot batis. The nest had blown down from the albida tree and the parent birds were still flying around, trying desperately to work out how to carry their chick and nest back to the top of the tree. There was no way, either for them, or us, as the trunk was completely devoid of any branches for at least ten metres and that was well out of reach of our ladder. There was however, a small scrubby bush growing underneath the albida, so Wayne decided to try and fix the nest into this shrub, hoping that the parent birds would accept the chick again, despite his having been handled.

Again it was the rainy season, so initially the nest was left out during the day, but taken in during the heavy storms so that the little bird did not get totally saturated too often, there being no parent bird to provide shelter. Wayne continued to feed it with pre-digested food and glucose water from an eye dropper and one day we noticed that shortly after the nest had been put back for the day, the parent birds started to visit it and bring in food for the chick. This dual feeding programme continued for about three days, until the chick was over the worst and then we left the natural parents to completely take over the task of feeding and caring for one very small, but fast growing, chinspot batis.

Appearances can be deceptive. Who would think that this punk rocker would develop into a regal Goliath heron? In order to obtain this photograph Jeff climbed the tree, the branch broke and he ended up like the chinspot batis — out of the nest.

Snapshots in the mind

We sometimes forget that the creatures around camp are not domestic stock raised by humans. So often when we are working we tend to almost ignore the game. This can become dangerous if taken it to extremes, but certainly if you ignore something as you walk past it *en route* to another area, it too seems to ignore or accept your presence and continues to browse or graze or ruminate without any interruption or hesitation.

This interaction has given me some of the most incredible photographic opportunities over the years. None of these are recorded except in my mind, but the recollection of a dozen pairs of waterbuck ears coming into view over the lip of the river bank, and moving in an orderly line towards the office where I was bashing away at the typewriter, is very vivid.

Do not disturb

Sapi, the resident elephant, was, like most bulls, wise, dignified and extremely tolerant of the human presence. So tolerant that on one occasion he walked within two metres of a guest who was lying asleep at the edge of the dining area. Sapi approached quietly, as elephant do, and there was simply no time to do anything but ensure that the man did not move as Sapi sauntered past him. We held our breath and the guest concerned obviously exercised a great deal of self-control, as apart from the barest flicker of an eyelid, he made no movement. He didn't even seem to be breathing, but once Sapi was safely past there was an explosion of movement as he hurried to the bar! This particular adrenalin seeker had met his match and achieved his "high".

Waterbuck breed year round, but tend to peak in February / March. As with impala, the young are sometimes left on their own, but usually form large herds. Their stance and gait are very distinctive and I am often reminded of a dowager duchess, mincing along in her high-heeled shoes.

Four legged road blocks

On a few occasions the early morning tea does not arrive and then we know that there is an elephant road block between us and the kitchen. More rare, but not unknown, are lion road blocks. Trying to expedite the delivery of early morning tea, Jeff once provided the staff and me with a great deal of amusement as he fled down the path, neck and neck with a male lion who was on the lower terrace. Both had failed to notice the presence of the other until it was really too late to retreat and both were desperately trying to reach safety and still maintain face. The camp staff were astounded by the turn of speed achieved by the Madala Mandebvu (the old man with a big beard and moustache).

Sounds of the wild

After our sense of sight has been assailed by the wilderness of Chikwenya, the next most obvious sense to be aroused is that of hearing. The sounds of the bush are very different from the sounds we are used to in a man-made environment, but not always more peaceful. Chikwenya can be a noisy place and not all the noises are soothing. Some sounds give you goose bumps and some make your hair stand on end. The noise factor that emanates from a large troop of baboon has to be heard to be appreciated. They vocalise loud and long and in an amazing number of different ways. Even soft sounds, when continuous, can be irritating. Animal noises, bird calls and the buzzings and cheepings of insects soon permeate our senses and become the accepted background noises, replacing the sounds of traffic, machinery or music.

Just as we have tried to blend into our surroundings, and not disrupt nature with an ugly picture of ourselves, so we try not to disturb the local inhabitants too much with our human noises and apart from the obvious necessity for the sounds of transport, we attempt to keep other mechanical noise to the minimum. This is one of the reasons for the rather limited light factor. The sound of the generator totally destroys the nocturnal concert.

A typical view of elephant - a baggy backside. Sapi on the path home. Many times I have had to make a detour to get to or from the radio room.

Good morning Chikwenya ... and goodnight

Each morning, the vocal efforts of our numerous bird species provide us with our own early alarm call. Not that we normally need alarms, as like all bush people, we wake up when it is light, glorying in the vista that is ours to behold each and every day. Often my eyes and throat ache with the beauty. The harsh call of the francolin is usually one of the first to register, but it is sometimes combined with the distant, booming echo of the ground hornbills. In the summer season, the Heuglin's robin provides the most glorious wake-up music, which is ever-melodic but always different, as he aspires to imitate the whole range of bird calls. On moonlight nights, the Egyptian geese honk incessantly. Dikkops, too, frequently call, with somewhat drawn out and plaintive cries. They are not normally a nocturnal species, but judging by the intensity of their calls, they suffer from moon madness. Seasonal changes are not confined to the weather. Crickets' chirps replace the tinkle of reed frogs and they in turn give way to the strident cicadas.

Helmetted guineafowl roost in trees near the dining area and seemingly cannot wait to get back to ground level each morning. They provide a slightly discordant note in the dawn chorus.

Female Egyptian geese honk in alarm while the males hiss when disturbed.

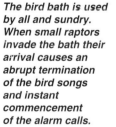

The bird bath is used by all and sundry. When small raptors invade the bath their arrival causes an abrupt termination of the bird songs and instant commencement of the alarm calls.

Crowned hornbill, for some reason, have become common in our area in recent years. They flop, rather than fly, from bush to bush, in a very clumsy manner.

81

Silence please

My best loved owl call is that belonging to the wood owl, which we often hear. Another frequent night sound is the somewhat monotonous series of grunts belonging to the giant eagle owl. One night we had a pair of these large owls close by, one on each side of the bedroom, and eventually, after being awakened time and time again, Jeff was driven to throw a shoe at them. There is a variation on the theme, from juvenile eagle owls. They utter a long drawn out and high pitched, squeaky door sound which descends the scale giving a bit of spice, and gingering up the by now, very monotonous grunting of the adult birds. I once spent hours wandering around the trees with a torch, trying to work out where this extraordinary noise was coming from. I saw the eagle owl, but refused to accept that such an unsuitable noise could possibly be coming from the largest-owl-of-them-all. After half an hour, I was forced to accept the evidence of both eyes and ears and returned to bed a lot colder and a bit wiser.

The problem with repeated calls is that one waits for the next series of grunts or wails, and the 'humph — hum hum hum' of the giant eagle owl ranks only second to the call of the side-striped jackal in the unpopularity poll, as far as Jeff is concerned. One night, in desperation, Jeff shouted down to Wayne, 'Turn it off!' But the, 'Yay, Yay, Yay,' continued unabated! Not unlike some pop songs.

Side striped jackal occur throughout the valley and, after keeping us awake all night, they make their way back to their dens in the early morning to rest up. They are not strictly nocturnal, but are seen most often at dawn and dusk, always moving with purpose. They scavenge off kills, but are low in the pecking order. The bulk of their diet consists of insects, small rodents and fruit.

The hippo's love song

In addition to the normal well-known grunts and blows, the hippo has a vast range of lesser-known vocalisations. Many a night's sleep has been broken up by what we call the hippo's love song. This can best be described as a series of wails and swooning sighs that range from one end of the scale to the other. Our assumption is not founded on fact at all. We just surmise that these extraordinary noises indicate extreme pleasure or pain. It is one of the things that I miss most when we leave camp. Somehow the series of low grunts from the hippos, both in and out of the water, is reassuring. It is never a sound that keeps one awake, but always there and normal. For us it acts both as a lullaby and as a wake-up call.

The very finely grained ivory tusks of hippo, although of limited size, play a vital role in territorial battles and reinforce the threatening gestures used by challenging hippopotami. The razor sharp edges are responsible for the extensive and bloody wounds which are seen when the loser retreats, out of the water, thus admitting defeat and loss of territory.

Sapi and the chopper

On the subject of noise, Sapi the elephant once exhibited the most extreme form of stress manifestation that we have ever seen. This was caused by total lack of thought on the part of a helicopter pilot seconded to the anti-poaching unit. He landed his helicopter really close to Sapi on the grassy area in front of camp. The elephant moved off and took shelter in the scrub. Eventually all was quiet, so he returned and continued grazing, only to be frightened yet again when the helicopter took off. Sapi had made the mistake of approaching too close to it while feeding, so again suffered from the full blast of noise and disturbance. Once again he rushed for shelter behind the camp and only returned after a couple of hours. His peace was to be shattered for a third time, as the helicopter had to return that evening, with a visitor from one of the conservation agencies who was staying with us. This final approach and landing was obviously intolerable. The elephant not only oozed from his temporal gland, but he actually squirted a strong jet of liquid, and screaming with fright, fled.

Unfortunately, we have never seen Sapi since. Sadly for him, the helicopter disturbance is now much more frequent than it was then, due to the use of helicopters by the game capture teams, and also the extensive helicopter surveys presently being undertaken as part of the search for oil in the Zambezi Valley. It is unlikely, therefore, that he can escape them forever, if at all.

The noise of a helicopter does seem to be unacceptable to game in general and to elephant in particular. No doubt they remember previous occasions, when members of their family were darted from the air and collared as part of the exercise to try and establish the range of the Zambezi Valley elephants.

The temporal gland in elephants often oozes. This is related to both stress and breeding conditions. Sapi's gland not only oozed or streamed, as is normal, but actually squirted, indicating his extreme stress, under unacceptable pressure which was brought to bear by the thoughtlessness of the chopper pilot.

Put the power on

Other familiar mechanical noises do not appear to cause the animals any distress or unease. Not a single head is lifted when the water pump is started and, during the latter months of the year Lovemore, our general duties hand, has to do a lot of ducking and diving and convoluted approaches to the water pump and the generator house, as the number of animal road blocks increases. The small group of Old Daga Boys, buffalo bulls who spend a lot of time in the mud a.k.a. daga, definitely favour the area immediately around the water pump for their afternoon siesta, and on the path to the generator there is an albida tree! Enough said! Elephant galore inhabit the area, and because we do not allow anybody to chase or harass them in camp, they spend the last half hour of daylight feasting on the ever-popular apple-ring pods which are now called 'Elephants' Biscuits' by our staff.

If the generator cannot be switched on, the chef cannot see

Daga — our name for mud. The elderly buffalo bulls, who no longer lead an active family life, seem to revel in mudbaths, which help to protect them against insect bites. It may be that some of the minerals in the mud act as repellants.

to continue his dinner preparations, the guests cannot see to have their showers, and the waiter is prevented from laying the tables. We all have to wait for the elephant to move off into the gloaming.

Because of these potential hazards, we have a number of detours and alternative routes to the strategic areas of the camp. I regularly make my way through the laundry lines and via the firewood pile at the back of the kitchen, in order to get to the radio room on time for our thrice daily schedule with the office in Kariba. Not every transmission is vital, but this radio is our only means of communication with the world outside Chikwenya. It enables us to place the food orders and organize the charter aircraft transfers, so we do try to maintain some sort of fairly regular contact, irrespective of road blocks. It certainly makes for a marvellously different storyline when one is late for work: 'Sorry I'm late, but there was an elephant on the path!' It also makes a change from the inevitable, 'I ran out of petrol', excuse!

Saucer, while demolishing part of our 'dining room walls', crushes a number of wild herbs and strong bush smells drift over the open area to my office, giving notice of the destruction.

Pungent and pleasant

Scents, of course, are a strong feature when one is in unfamiliar surroundings. Certainly the bush presents us with a whole new collection of smells. I suspect that we often do not care to use our noses in town as many 'fragrances' are far from pleasant. Chikwenya abounds with its own particular smells, which for me are very atmospheric, and it also has plenty of smells which are all about Africa.

Buffalo, I feel, have the most evocative smell — it is surely the original 'dark brown' smell of Africa and this seems to be accentuated when these beasts are in or near water. It is not only the smell of their dung, but their body smell as well and I freely admit to a tendency to get down on my hands and knees to get closer to what represents for me the primitive, sweaty scent of the wild. It is not a subtle scent like that of the first rains, which is carried tantalizingly on the wind, but is a solid, down to earth, no nonsense smell.

Buffalo herds on occasions number up to five hundred beasts and certainly leave behind a farmyard smell when they have passed through an area. Lingering dust and shiny, floppy, wet pats are often the only indication that the big herd was there.

87

That 'first rains' smell is unique to Africa. It can only occur in a land where one has prolonged, dry, hot periods and indeed many droughts. It is the smell of hope and continuance. Even if the rain falls many kilometres away, the smell pervades the entire valley and we all stop and face into the wind, with our noses twitching, rather like gun dogs seeking the scent of the bird.

The earth smells vary too, from the dry, dusty, irritating smell of October, to the smell of land revitalized after the first shower of rain. More pungent, but no less attractive, is the smell of soil which is saturated with urine and then dampened by a few drops of rain. The same odour is produced when the river rises, inundating the usually dry river terraces, which are covered with urine and dung deposits.

The hot smells come when it is warm and muggy. They should be the freshest smells in the bush, but sometimes the air is just so still, and the perfumes from the blossoms are so cloyingly sweet, that they are sickening.

The cold smells are less easy to pinpoint. There is just the faintest whiff of dampness in the pre-dawn when the sun has not yet burnt off the dew; and this, intermingled with the campfire smell, which has been part of our lives for ever, is amazingly atmospheric. Even in the middle of town when someone burns a piece of mopane wood, in a flash we are back in the valley, eagerly awaiting the first cup of slightly smoky tea and watching the sun as it spills over the buildings and throws long shadows, reaching across the Sapi and the floodplain.

This woodsmoke appeal of the campfire is common all over the world and, I believe, is one of the links with our less sophisticated and more real past lives, when we were totally dependent on the campfire for warmth, protection and for the preparation of our meals.

The mention of meals brings to mind the glorious mouth-watering smell of a good piece of steak being grilled on an open fire, as well as the farmyard kitchen smell of bread baking. We still make all our bread at Chikwenya, so daily are faced with the temptation of trying to refuse the delectable, still oven-hot, bread rolls and scones. Most people succumb with glee and dedication.

The glorious sight of a Coffea in full bloom. One day of splendour and then it reverts to a twiggy, stubby, stunted shrub. The scent is very subtle and delicate. Botanists are trying to propagate the wild coffea, in order that its disease-resistant properties can be used to advantage in the field of agricultural production, as it is of the same family as cultivated coffee.

The bush herbarium

Other smells which bring to mind food and cooking, are those of the wild herbs, basil, thyme and rosemary to name a few. We immediately move out of the kitchen and into the sanatorium, when the wheels of a vehicle crush a plant of *Ocinum,* either with its euchalyptus smell or its clove-like aroma, which for me is reminiscent of the sick-bay and tooth-ache rather than the kitchen and apple pie.

My complete lack of domestic skills is the reason behind what must seem to be a horrible waste of a natural resource, in that we do not use any of the wild herbs. I am not sure how they should be treated or prepared to bring out their natural flavours. I have also given a passing thought to the fact that I might just pluck something poisonous in a fit of misguided enthusiasm. Elias, who is one of our room staff, is a registered herbalist and he has a good knowledge of many of the natural remedies which are available to us. He seeks out roots and seeds and pieces of bark from a vast variety of plants and grinds them down to fine powders which are kept in traditional cattle-horn containers. On the drive in and out of the valley, whenever we stop for puncture repairs or to cut back fallen trees, Elias disappears into the bush in search of something special. I have discussed with him the use of these herbal medicines and was amused to note, that from the outset, he stated that there were certain things he could not cure and old age was one of them!

We do occasionally try to get guests involved in the 'how to survive in the veld' scene but this is difficult to pursue with any degree of enthusiasm when you know that there will be only half ripe fruits, which are going to be sour enough to make your mouth pucker for days on end, and even cause toothache, gasps of horror, loss of breath and streaming eyes!

It is the baboon and vervet monkey who really prevent us from being able to enjoy the wild fruits, as they always get to them before us, and rightly so, as they need them to survive, whereas we are just playing at it.

There are two schools of thought as to whether one should or whether one should not serve venison in a photographic safari camp. We don't for a number of reasons; firstly it has to be really well-butchered, prepared and cooked as otherwise it is just too gamey; secondly, we both feel that the guests are at Chikwenya to look at the game, not to eat it; thirdly, and probably the main real reason, is that Jeff and I don't like it.

The river could provide us with delicious and delicate tasting bream, which is the common name for all species of tilapia, but due to the volume of guests, we have to compromise and buy fish from a commercial fishing camp in Kariba. It would not be possible for us to catch enough bream on rod and line to feed all the guests, and all Jeff's fishing skills are employed in catching fish for the fish eagle which, after all, is much more important.

No cabbage patch

Most people are surprised that we do not grow our own fruit or vegetables. I used to try, but found that the endless battle against the insects, and the mindless task of trying to stop a dozen different species of game from enjoying the fresh growth, was too much trouble to be really worthwhile. In any event, these plants are not indigenous to the valley and can spread way beyond the confines of one's garden. We have an excellent example in the very large and healthy banana plant growing on Chikwenya Island! We have caused enough of a disturbance simply by living in the valley and have no wish to intrude further by erecting high fences, digging steep ditches, or spraying toxic insecticides and herbicides. All of these unsuitable actions would be necessary if we wanted to grow fruit and vegetables, so we obtain all our supplies from Harare.

The destructive sausage

The nearest shops are in Kariba, but the choice of goods is limited. Shopping by radio is therefore the easiest method of obtaining what we need. The range of our requirements is quite extensive and certainly varied. This particular aspect of operating a safari camp can also cause amusement to the other users of the 'open' radio network. This must certainly have been the case on the occasion I went 'on set' to order a replacement toilet seat. The inevitable occurred and it was queried. 'How did you manage to break the seat?' Answer, 'It got hit by a falling sausage.' A long pause and then the request to, 'Say again?' I repeated the message slowly.

The full explanation is that Hut Number 8 is built adjacent to a large and prolific sausage tree. The fruits grow to incredible sizes and often fall when we have a heavy wind. The reason for my urgent need of a new toilet set was that one such large and heavy fruit had fallen from a height of some five metres on to the loo and shattered the seat. Thank goodness nobody was in residence at the time! The terminal velocity of a ten kilogram missile would surely be enough to crack a skull as easily as a seat!

Warthog are the clowns of the bush and, while appealing, could never be called attractive with their warts protruding below the eyes and above the tushes. Generally seen as a small family unit, Ma, Pa and two piglets, the young are born in mid-November and often grace the table of bush dwellers as 'suckling pig'. Their feeding method is to root out under-ground tubers and roots and in order to do this, they adopt a comical stance — knees down and bums up. There are what we call 'warthog gardens' developing in the Vetevaria, where bare patches are caused by warthog uprooting the vegetation.

Hooked on the bush

The knowledge, or lack of it as the case may be, as to what constitutes suitable clothing, often gives us a laugh or causes embarrassment. Jeff has never been a follower of fashion trends, either for himself or for women. For this reason he did not quite appreciate the extent of the damage he caused one day. He had collected a group of five guests from the airstrip and, as usual, decided to give them a short introductory game drive on the way to camp. Our roads are mere tracks and, by August, the long, spiny tendrils of the *Combretum obovatum* are spreading and extending across the tracks to hook into the clothing of unwary guests. We always give a warning, but on this occasion the new guest either did not hear it or did not heed it. Jeff swung round a corner, a branch of the combretum snatched at her blouse and with a definite rending sound her sleeve parted company from the rest of her blouse. Not really serious, thought Jeff. What he did not know, and could never really appreciate anyway, was that it was a Gucci silk blouse.

The feel of things on our skin is possibly the last of our senses to be stimulated. Having said this, I must make mention of the immediate reaction we get from the guests when they experience their first tsetse fly bite. This usually occurs as they drive from the airstrip to camp, and it is a sharp reminder that they are now in the bush. Tsetse bites are sore and irritating, but not lethal. They should, in fact, be welcomed, as the fly are considered to be the supreme conservator. Their continued presence in wildlife areas ensures the long-term survival of the game. Where there are tsetse fly, no domestic stock survive. For this reason, wildlife lovers with a grand passion for the valley, should certainly not complain when bitten by the tsetse fly. The incidence of trypanosomiasis in humans is negligible these days and a few welts are a small price to pay for the revitalising experience of being at Chikwenya. Mosquito bites, which really only cause discomfort during the rains, are merely an irritant, easily controlled by repellents. How vital and energising it is to have our faces in the wind as we drive through the woodland in search of wildlife. What a marvellous cleansing we get from the feel of the first raindrops at the end of a long, hot summer, as they wash away the dry, gritty dust.

The tactile nature of Chikwenya is reinforced when, with trepidation to be sure, you stick your finger into a warm ball of elephant dung. This is how we gauge its age and from that the guide works out how far ahead the beast may be. It is possibly this practice that has led to the phrase, 'hot on the tracks'.

During the morning walks, a much more intense feeling of the wild is gained by accepting the guide's recommendation to feel the texture of a particular leaf or bloom and to willingly, or unwillingly, feel the scratchy texture of some of the grass seeds or thorny branches while exploring the land!

Surely these minor irritants cannot compare with the enormously gratifying feeling of having been in the bush, in the flesh, able to see, hear, smell, taste and feel.

Strophanthus combe is a leggy, spindly creeping plant which has a classic seed dispersal system. The large brown moustache-shaped pods split open and the wind stirs the seeds, each of which has its own parachute to assist its flight. The reaching tendrils are just one of the many hazards on the way back from the airstrip.

Overleaf: In contrast to the usual red and orange backgrounds, elephant in silhouette against a silvery blue backdrop, creating a spiritual and other-worldly atmosphere.

The core of the camp

Jumping for joy

In our area we are blessed with a wide variety of bird and animal life, exceptions being the species that require a specific habitat, such as the 'plains game'. Some species are more plentiful and visible than others. In Zimbabwe as a whole, and certainly in the Zambezi Valley, impala are the most common antelope. This does not detract from their appeal and beauty. In addition to their beautiful bodies and very rich colouring, a large part of their attraction stems from their overall attitude.

I firmly believe that impala jump for joy. There are many occasions when we are sitting quietly observing a mixed herd of rams, does and yearlings when, simultaneously and without any apparent cause, they leap into the air, pirouette gracefully without effort and then come to earth again to return to the never-ending task of feeding. When in flight there is reason enough for every beast to fully extend itself; seeking safety from predators and to escape from the overbearing attentions of visitors crammed into assorted Land Rovers. When vehicles approach too closely, the impala stand stock still, then suddenly, with minimum effort and maximum grace, they leap high — all four legs extended to reach even further and reduce the resistance by streamlining their overall shape. In mid-air we often see that they tend to give a final kick with their rear legs, which we assume adds a little more impetus to their jump for joy.

The impala lambs are exquisite. Delicately formed and with stick-like legs still wobbly, their heads initially appear far too big for their bodies. With anticipation, we always await the first sighting of the impala lambs at the end of each season, pondering how it is that within a few hours they are running swiftly and surely with the herd. Naturally we know that they have to be able to evade the predators, and so this again is part of the survival-of-the-fittest rule which prevails in the wild. When we compare the feeble, puny efforts of a newborn human infant, it again reinforces the fact that our instinctive responses and reactions are atrophying at an alarming rate. This is the result of today's lifestyle and due, in no small part, to the fact that we generally have everything provided with the minimum of effort. A consequence of this easy-to-get situation

Impala rams frequently jump at least two metres off the ground in a grand show of exhilaration. This style of jump, from a standing start, must burn up a great deal of energy, but it does not deter them. As a species, they seem to be full of restless energy and rarely seem to relax.

is that people lose a great deal of their ingenuity, some of their spirit of adventure, and sadly, they also lose their *joie de vivre*. Eventually they are unable to jump for joy. We so often despair of those visitors who cannot find the time or make the effort to look at yet another impala. After all these years, Jeff still stops time and time again. His enthusiasm has never diminished and very often his delight and great excitement far exceed the guests' reactions. Maybe it is a case of familiarity not breeding contempt, but reverence, for the life all around us.

The breeding patterns of impala place a strain on the dominant male, who has to remain in control at all times. He must always be alert for any sign of danger in the form of predators waiting in ambush in the thick Vetevaria. Often he has up to fifty does to protect — no mean task.

Animal creche

Once all the impala lambs have dropped, the mothers develop a nursery system and often we find up to twenty lambs lying quietly under a tree with one doe in charge and on guard. She will lead them back to their mothers and safety if danger threatens and we assume that this temporary, off-duty time allows the other does to graze and browse further afield on a much greater variety of vegetation, enabling them to produce sufficient quality milk for their young.

At the end of October there is not a great deal of fresh, nutritious feed to be found in the valley and it is the impala who exhibit the most visible signs of malnutrition. They develop mange, a skin disease which is carried by a mite and is prevalent amongst animals that are undernourished and in poor condition. It seems bad planning that they have to carry their young all through the hot, dry months, but the master plan is sound. They produce sufficient good food for their offspring from the wholesome and highly nutritious annual grasses which become available about a week after the first heavy rainfall.

It is usual to see the first impala lamb between the middle and end of November. If the rains are late, then they manage to retain their young for a considerable period of time. In Hwange some time ago, there was a severe drought and the arrival of the impala young was delayed until just two days before Christmas. This was a direct result of the first substantial rain, sufficient to germinate the buried grass seeds, only falling well after mid-December. For a smallish antelope, impala have a long, seven month pregnancy and the sometimes alarming, totally out of character sounds of their rutting in May cause a goodly number of people to question what they are hearing.

The males rush around in ever decreasing circles, compelled to vie for the breeding females and become the dominant ram with his 'harem' herd. Having achieved his objective, for the remainder of the year the ram is sore pressed to control up to fifty does who all need to be serviced, as well as protected and occasionally disciplined. It is not surprising that this dominance and control of the breeding herd only lasts for a couple of years before he is ousted by a younger, more virile ram. The bachelor herds of impala, therefore, consist of both young and old rams — the youngsters all hopeful that in time they will gain dominance and some of the old men, no doubt, reflecting on their past glories.

Baboon watching

For many years I have stuck to the firm conclusion that wild animals act only on instinct. Having said this, I make an exception as far as baboon are concerned. There is absolutely no doubt in my mind that they plan to do things which they know will cause mayhem. Many hours of baboon observation through my office window — little wonder that sometimes the books do not balance — have led me to conclude that they can reason. However, their reasoning most certainly does not prevent them from often creating absolute chaos.

Most people seem to accept that part of their appeal lies in the fact that they are so similar to man. However, they are surely much less inhibited than we, more freely expressing joy, desire, hunger, thirst, anger, aggression or even alarm. The alarm calls of primates and antelope repay attention and

the distinctive alarm bark of baboon can lead to the discovery of the predatory cat. It is not always easy. Baboon and monkey perch in the tallest trees and so have the advantage of height,

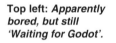
Top left: *Apparently bored, but still 'Waiting for Godot'.*

Top right: *Bomb-shelling without checking up to see why.*

Bottom left: *Their varied diet includes fruit from a sausage tree for breakfast.*

Bottom right: *Always alert and extra wary when drinking.*

as well as superior vision. But by spending time following the direction of their eyes and noting the direction in which the impala are pointing, perseverance pays. The reward of the sight of a leopard quietly walking through the clumps of *Vetevaria,* or a lion crossing the dry river bed in indolent fashion, is incomparable.

The huge, male dog baboon are awesome when they stand and scream at you, with their enormous yellow fangs displayed to advantage. Display, as we now know, is a major part of defensive behaviour. If you can stand up on your two back legs and wave your arms high in the air and screech loud and long, the potential threat is less likely to develop. This tactic has been adopted by many a safari guide and hunter who has found himself in a situation potentially dangerous to his clients. The rule is, stand tall, make a loud noise and most important, do not back down or run away. Everyone and everything should avoid confrontations, if possible, and these threat displays which can be so terrifying are intended to persuade you that discretion is the better part of valour. The more one watches the behaviour of wildlife, the more one deplores the actions of man.

Baboon are certainly amusing, and they are also rather 'street-wise' and often foul up our final approach for the ultimate photograph with a loud, derisive, 'Wahoo!', causing everything in the area to scatter. It seems to me that they glance over their backsides in a truly gloating manner as if to say, 'Tough! Try again.'

One behavioural trait which causes me to doubt their wisdom is their habit of bombshelling out of a tree as one approaches, either in a vehicle or on foot. I feel sure they must recognize that we are poor climbers and can present absolutely no threat to them if they remain perched high in the branches of a tall tree. It seems that the only reasonable answer is that they feel that they could be trapped 'out on a limb', so to speak, but there is also the danger that they would not be able to remain 'out on a limb', as they are large, heavy animals and the ends of high branches are not very substantial. Vervet monkey, on the other hand, do take to the trees when they feel threatened, and either take refuge right at the very top or utilise their incredible balance and agility to leap across great distances to the next tree and the next one after that and so escape.

One of the most poignant sights in the bush is that of a female baboon carrying around with her, for days, the body of her dead baby. It is heartbreaking to watch as she follows the normal behaviour when starting to move off, instinctively clamping her youngster underneath her belly. It would normally grip on to her hair and teats and be carried safely as the troop proceed, either at a fast pace if trying to escape from potential danger or, at a more leisurely pace if feeding. The mother does not seem to realize that the baby is unattached and goes along for a couple of metres before turning slowly back to pick it up again. Fondling the baby, she seems to inspect it and then the whole sad sequence is repeated. I have no idea if this behaviour is common in first-time mothers only, or whether it is perhaps peculiar to older mothers who are reaching the end of their productive years. From the observations we have made, there does not seem to be any common factor except that the baby is dead and is carried around for as long as three days before finally being abandoned.

Via the river

All animals can swim; their expertise or lack of it became noticeable during the 'Operation Noah' game rescue on Lake Kariba. However, some species prefer not to swim if they can avoid it. It is for this reason that on Chikwenya Island there are good populations of bushbuck, who are strong swimmers, living in the shady, well-timbered woodlands at the western end of the island. It is noticeable when first climbing from the boat to walk on the island that there is a very low browse line. The reason for this is that it is a bushbuck browse line rather than a kudu browse line and we have to bend twice as low under the trees as we do when walking on the mainland. For some reason, kudu do not occur on the island and neither do warthog, nor zebra. This is probably because they are not good or enthusiastic swimmers, but elephant are and they frequently cross to and fro, as do the smaller groups of buffalo bulls.

The vista greeting us each morning is nothing short of spectacular in itself, without the added bonus of lying in bed, drinking a cup of tea, watching a family group of elephant swimming across the river from Chikwenya Island. The breeding herds get excited and noisy when about to embark on a major river crossing. We not only see them wading, swimming and even snorkelling, but we also hear their uncharacteristic squeals. When they emerge from the water, they are unsettled and generally hurry off to the shelter of the thicket, forming a single file of great, dark beasts with gleaming ivory, moving purposefully across the open floodplain.

Despite their initial hesitancy when confronted with a puddle of water, lion too swim surprisingly strongly and so the canoeists, who camp on islands in the mistaken belief that they will be totally safe from predators, often get a horrible shock. There are seven lion resident on Chikwenya Island. Monkeys do not occur, which is strange as they are really good swimmers and in fact dive below the surface of the water and do breaststroke rather than the normal animal paddle! Baboon, however, simply hate to get wet and the few that occur are probably descendants of the original population which was isolated when the island was cut off from the mainland.

For some years there has been a very large breeding herd of buffalo living on Chikwenya Island, which explains the presence of lion there and they provide us and our guests with spectacular sights as they stampede across the sandbars plunging through the shallows and creating amazingly substantial bow waves, which rock the boat for a few minutes after their passage. This large herd does not migrate back to the mainland, but the Old Daga Boys regularly toddle across the shallows to graze on the smaller, grassy islands.

Elephant making their way across the river to feed on Chikwenya Island. Generally they stay there for a few days, but occasionally may travel even further into Zambia. The pattern that has developed seems to be afternoon crossings to the island and early morning returns.

Sometimes, instead of just wading, the elephant have to swim across the deep channels. When they submerge, they keep their trunks high and constantly scent so they do not lose direction. The rich, late afternoon light shows up the muscle ridges on the undersides of the trunks. In order to control the trunk and make effective use of it, elephants have a complex muscular trunk structure.

Leave me some

Bull elephants are normally the individuals with whom we become most familiar. They come into camp regularly, unhesitatingly visiting the trees which are a source of food. Inside their brain must be the most enormous road map in the world, showing where food is to be found in which season. I am convinced it is not just the smell of the ripening fruit which attracts them, as we have watched a totally strange and unknown elephant approach an albida tree secure in the knowledge that it is a source of food.

Another definite habit of elephant, in fact of a number of species, is that they never completely finish all the food that is available. We tend to criticise, saying they waste a lot and this may be true, but at other times, when we watch the impala approaching to take advantage of the elephants' left-overs, understanding slowly dawns. Perhaps it is not a question of waste, but in fact of providing for others of the species, as well as for the other inhabitants of the valley. This generosity, deliberate or otherwise, often backfires.

Imagine this scenario. One of the big bulls breaks a huge branch of albida full of leaves and pods. He eats sparingly, leaving much of the food on the ground and moves off. After he has left it, two younger elephant bulls appear from nowhere, rushing to take advantage of this unexpected feast. They in turn wander off and then the remains are enjoyed by the impala and bushbuck who, like all wild animals, are not averse to eating left-overs. Is this planned? Do they know what they are doing when they wander off, having sometimes only eaten two or three trunkfuls of food? I am never quite certain. Doubt creeps in when we notice that the same elephant will sometimes return to that tree an hour or so, or even a day or so later, searching for the branch covered with leaves and pods

that was left behind. The smaller antelope and even the smaller elephant cannot handle the large and thick branches, so these at least are always still there for the original procurer to chew in a meditative fashion. Anthropomorphism is abhorrent amongst the scientific community, but in recent years the study of ethology, animal behaviour, has led to a slight relaxing of the stringent set of rules which used to be applied. Over a number of years, these field studies have thrown up some extremely interesting and unexpected data and behaviour patterns. While we have benefited enormously from the many books and papers on elephant behaviour, we suffer from a dearth of material on hippopotamus. Nevertheless, we fully appreciate that intensive study of an amphibious beast, which spends the daytime hours in crocodile infested waters and the night-time hours wandering as far as fifteen kilometres inland in search of grazing, would not be easy!

Due to the very regular visits of mature elephant bulls, we have often been unable to descend from our tree-house bedroom because one of them is at the foot of the ladder,

Elephant and impala seem unlikely candidates for a close relationship, but these impala are feeding quite at ease on the bits and pieces that the bull elephant has discarded. The proximity of the buck provokes no reaction from the elephant.

102

calmly collecting and eating the albida pods. This is fascinating to watch as it involves the full use of the 'finger' at the end of an elephant's trunk and also a little tossing motion, followed by a brief exhalation when the apple-ring pod is literally blown into the enormous mouth. When the elephant bulls feed high we have the unique opportunity to observe the inside of their mouths at close quarters and believe me the size of an elephant's epiglottis is amazing!

If other elephant were to approach as close as these impala, it is most unlikely that Saucer would show such tolerance and allow them to share his left-overs in so generous a manner.

A hide in the house

Often guests feel sorry for me being left in camp. Little do they know that I welcome the peace and quiet and also have my own private game-viewing 'hide' in the house. One hot, August afternoon a family of cheetah were seen on the floodplain. It seemed too hot for them to kill, but they stalked and successfully brought down an impala ram. Wayne and I were watching, enthralled by the sight of that specialised hunting movement — legs and body fully extended and visibly gaining in length — with the large, bushy tail moving from side to side and acting as a rudder. With the incredible burst of speed over, the adults completed the kill and then lay panting for at least ten minutes while the two young started to feed greedily. We let them feed without disturbance and then walked over to check what remained of the carcase. This time they had managed to get a good meal and the bulk of the meat was consumed. It had taken only twenty minutes and as we approached vultures were already gathering to squabble over the meagre remains.

What superb design can be seen in the specifically adapted body formation of the cheetah. Long body, deep chest, small head, long legs and bushy tail all play a vital role in the hunting method. Such specialisation does restrict the distribution, as cheetah need wide open spaces and do not operate effectively in heavily wooded areas.

Elusive visitors

While we have regular and frequent sightings of lion, my favourite cat is the cheetah. The range of the cheetah is vast and the individuals we see roam the entire Mana Pools National Park right up to the Rukomechi camp about seventy kilometres away. Marginal in the valley, the few occasions on which we see them become more special.

One year there was a family of four and we saw them a number of times in the woodland. Cheetah are sensitive and easily chased from their kills. Often the only evidence we had that they were still around was a half-eaten impala. The young male cheetah broke his leg, presumably whilst racing around on the broken up and elephant pot-holed areas and he subsequently died. After this the family moved off for the remainder of that year. We see cheetah each year but recently it seems always to be at the beginning of the season in April or May. Perhaps they just keep clear of the wild dog which seem to become more visible towards the end of the season. Having seen the cheetah family in 1986, we felt sure it was the remaining offspring we saw in 1987, who accomplished her first visible kill alone.

There are always impala in sight, even at the hottest time of the day, and the cheetah lolled in the shade of a tree on the banks of the Sapi and allowed the small herd to approach closer and closer. Suddenly, with no prior indication that she was hunting, she literally exploded into action and managed to catch an impala. It was not a very clean kill and the impala got up a couple of times and staggered off, but kill it the cheetah eventually did and fed successfully without being intimidated by any other predators. For some reason we tend to identify more with a lone animal and we all shared the sense of achievement.

The regal dignity of the cheetah was totally compromised on another occasion. This time a young male was lying in the sandy river bed of the Sapi, basking in the early morning sun. There is always a great gathering of baboon and they frequently cross to and fro, usually with large males not only in the lead but also bringing up the rear of the troop. All appeared normal and the greater part of the troop had passed by the cheetah, when abruptly, six or so of the brash young males separated from the main troop. Banding together, they put on the 'heavies' act, advancing menacingly in a line. The cheetah tried to retain his dignity and remain in control, but finally he had to bow down to the intimidation and ran off into the *Vetevaria*. He was not seen again that year so his pride must have been terribly hurt.

Living with the leopard

Undoubtedly the supreme predator is the leopard. They are almost impossible to see unless they choose to show themselves during daytime. Night-time drives with a spotlight prove to be productive in certain areas, most especially in the Luangwa National Park in Zambia. We have a good leopard population, we have good leopard calls, we have good spoor to be seen daily going through the dining area, but we do not have good leopard viewing. The exception is on the few occasions when Jeff and I are fortunate enough to have the big tom leopard come to drink at the birdbath at home. During the dry months everything drinks at the birdbath except the birds who do not get a chance. The first time I saw the leopard, I was sitting with an evening drink. In my excitement I nearly dropped the drink, but I was so worried about disturbing him that my whisper did not reach Jeff inside. However, I need not have bothered to whisper. This leopard had been around a long time, knew the place much better than we did, and was totally unconcerned about us.

A frequent visitor, he is not predictable as far as timing goes, but we often see him while we are changing for dinner or having a quiet drink at home before showering. Sometimes we hear him drinking during the night and get up and shine the torch on him and watch with delight. Taking a long time to quench his thirst, usually about eight or nine minutes, he is so tolerant that he not only allows us to move about and fetch binoculars or a bigger torch, but he also waits as Jeff stumbles around trying to set up the tripod and focus the big lens, a torch in one hand and binoculars in the other, glasses slipping off the end of his nose! But flash photography is a specialised art and so far our efforts have not proved to be of the best

The chances of getting a portrait-type shot of a leopard in the wild are unlikely, but Jeff's patience and high expectations were rewarded, much to his delight. Usually leopard sightings are of the flash-and-blur type and more often than not these elusive creatures are seen by spotlight.

quality. Anyway I want to absorb the sight without worrying about focus or the light in the eye!

Despite the fact that leopard are lethal and efficient killers, I never feel the hairs on my neck rise when in close proximity to them, as I do when close to lion. There are many times however, when I am almost numb with delight. One very special time for me was when I was on my own. Jeff was in Australia promoting the country and the camp. Returning from dinner, I was pottering around getting ready for bed when I

106

heard a series of growls. 'Gosh those lion are close but they sound strange,' I thought. I went upstairs and sat on the verandah to watch. It was full moon and I frequently spend time watching as it seems a crime to waste the moonlight. The intensity of the growls increased, the frequency definitely increased and formed a pattern, and then out of the *Vetevaria*, appeared the big male leopard followed by a very pretty, small, dark female. They were totally engrossed in each other and the growls I had heard had been the normal feline 'completion' calls. I watched, absolutely spellbound, for about twenty minutes until they slowly moved out of sight and disappeared. I felt very privileged, but also desperately sorry that Jeff had not been there to share it with me, especially as he hated every moment confined to hotel rooms, lifts and aircraft, in endless rounds of talks, presentations, seminars and slide shows.

Gory evidence is sometimes all that is seen of leopard kills. In common with all other cats, they disembowel their prey and very often bury, or at least cover the stomach contents, to prevent the smell from attracting other predators or scavengers.

Below right: A partially eaten impala ram again reinforces the widely-accepted theory of males being the favoured prey. Over the years, at least ninety percent of the kills we have seen or found have been rams. Another interesting point is that the heavily-muscled and blood-filled haunches are eaten first, ensuring the greatest immediate return of energy to the predator.

Leopard larder

Many people see lion killing, but few see leopard kills. Being nocturnal and more secretive, they generally keep to the denser bush not often operating on the open grasslands. Again, on a magical moonlight night we heard and saw our big male leopard kill an impala on the floodplain in front of the house. The impala alarm calls were loud and clear and eventually continuous. We were alerted to the fact that there was a predator around. Even with the moon casting good light, it was difficult to discover the leopard, but eventually we found him with the aid of the big torch and binoculars, and watched as he killed an impala ram. A short, quick run, a brief struggle and it was all over.

He disembowelled the beast and then fed before he proceeded to drag it away and stash it in the fork of the mahogany tree at the entrance to the dining area! It was mid-winter and we were freezing so eventually we went back to bed. Early next morning, we checked to see if we had been hallucinating. No, definitely not, the carcase was still there, partially eaten and lodged about five metres up the tree!

Anticipating fantastic viewing that night, when the leopard returned to feed, we were disappointed that a vehicle breakdown thwarted us. The afternoon game drive stretched into an evening, then eventually into a night drive! By the time Jeff had walked back to camp from the farthest point in our area, and by the time we had towed the wretched Toyota home, it was far too late for leopard watching. The cat had been, had fed and was gone and only the staff had been lucky enough to watch from the safety of the bar counter! However, there was still a lot of meat left on the carcase so we knew that he would return to feed again.

I was becoming a little concerned about a leopard feeding in a tree in the dining area, within ten metres of our guests, so I persuaded Jeff to move the kill down and on to the floodplain, where it would be not only more visible, but also more distant. This was duly done, although I know Jeff felt I was creating an unnecessary fuss. The final act of the drama was still to take place. Sure enough, the leopard did return to his kill and fed in the moonlight with everyone watching. Then, having had sufficient, he returned the carcase to its original location in the mahogany tree at the entrance to the dining area!

I then accepted that the whole situation was beyond my control and resigned myself to having a now smelly carcase in the 'dining room' and also to having a leopard feeding on that carcase while we were having dinner. This was not a problem but, incredible as it may seem, there was more to come.

The next night, after turning off the generator, we were on our way back home when we spotted the leopard climbing up the tree to feed. This time he was not alone as another cat appeared. The leopard was being followed by a young lioness. She was desperately trying to climb the tree and get at what remained of the impala! Lion do not climb as well as leopard and the trunk was too steep for her, but for a couple of hours there was a chorus of growls and hisses and huffs and puffs as she repeatedly leapt up and fell back. The next morning, large and deep scratch marks proved that we had seen what we thought we had seen and I managed to persuade Jeff to remove the last bits and pieces of the kill.

So there are leopard at Chikwenya, but we have to work hard to see them and accept the flash and blur sightings with thanks. One of our longstanding clients had to wait eighteen

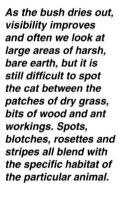

As the bush dries out, visibility improves and often we look at large areas of harsh, bare earth, but it is still difficult to spot the cat between the patches of dry grass, bits of wood and ant workings. Spots, blotches, rosettes and stripes all blend with the specific habitat of the particular animal.

years before he saw a leopard in the wild and in his excitement he forgot to take any photographs, even though the sighting was in full daylight and on open ground.

Those of us who are interested in observing all aspects of animals' lifestyles accept that we must continue our observations into the night. This is not always easy, mainly because, unlike animals, we cannot see well at night, but one period which I feel is frequently neglected is the time of the full moon. The nights in the bush are the time when one needs to be wide awake and alert, as it is a time of increased activity, not only among the predators, who definitely come into their own, but also among the antelope. The cool of the evening gives them respite from the day's heat and encourages more and faster movement. Humans are at such a disadvantage at night, with vision restricted to the circle of light thrown by the torch, hampering observation and understanding.

I have made many references to my 'moon madness', or to incidents which occurred during the full moon period and I make no apology for another. This particular story relates to hyena. Generally speaking hyena are not popular animals, but

Large numbers of buffalo on the move cause so much dust that they create a ghostly atmosphere.

recently it has been proved that they most definitely are predators, not only scavengers. In some areas it has also been found that lion scavenge on hyena kills more than they actually hunt for themselves.

On the moonlight night in question, a large breeding herd of about four hundred buffalo was working its way out of the thicket and across the floodplain towards the river. The well-known and somewhat eerie, 'Whooee', of the hyena was heard. The call was picked up from beyond the Sapi, repeated yet again from the woodland and suddenly there was a highly organised pack of hunters. In all, seven hyena answered the original call, which must have been instantly understood as the response was very quick.

The buffalo herd was scattered and peacefully grazing with many calves spread out and not, as sometimes happens, tightly clustered at its centre. The hyena movements were economical and designed to harass the chosen cow, edging her away from her calf long enough for the kill to be effected. It took some time, as buffalo are not easily intimidated and many an advance by the hyena deteriorated into ignominious retreat, tails tucked between legs, as the buffalo charged them.

The tempo of the chase increased and their vocalisations changed. Now it was no longer, 'Whooee', but we began to hear the giggles and laughs as the pack developed their hunting and feeding frenzy. This I am told, stimulates them, as well as frightening the prey animal and it is truly terrifying to the ear.

Persisting and pursuing their chosen victim, the hyena passed in front of the house and over the sandy river bed where, with a sudden, concerted rush, they succeeded in isolating the calf from its mother and the hunt was complete.

The plumbers

Another nocturnal visitor which gives us an enormous amount of pleasure and amusement is the honey badger. Over the years we have had a constant stream of them coming to visit the kitchen drain. It seems that they thrive on grease and spend many happy hours scooping it up out of the greasetrap. It is disgusting to watch and no doubt, when combined with copious quantities of detergent, extremely damaging to their gut. One drought year, we watched what I think was the most horrendous sight I have ever seen. Although it is not usual, lion had killed a couple of honey badger and when we heard an ear-splitting screech of agony the next night, we knew that another badger had been attacked. We rushed back to the kitchen in the Land Rover and saw a large lioness near the firewood pile with 'Old Man' in her jaws. He was struggling valiantly, scratching and clawing at her, but it was an unequal struggle and he died after forty five long minutes.

I was so distressed that I became irrational and urged Jeff to shoot the lioness. I was also secretly delighted to see that she was severely wounded under her neck and chin and lower chest area, by his claws. It seemed so unnecessary for her to kill him, but one can only assume that she had now developed a taste for badger and was also taking advantage of their habitual visits to the kitchen. Honey badger are strong, formidable creatures and very plucky. Their coats are thick and loose, normally giving them some measure of protection from bees when they raid the hives, but not from lion.

The odd couple

I will always treasure the memory of another very unusual sighting we had during our early years at Chikwenya. Again, taking advantage of the moonlight, we were watching a hippo grazing and listening to the endless repetitious, 'Chomp, chomp, chomp,' when a rhino quietly appeared from the thicket behind the house and browsed its way close to the hippo. The difference in size was outstanding, as was the totally different body formation and overall aspect. Obviously each knew the other was there although no acknowledgement was made. Beautifully backlighted by the moon, which gave them an other-worldly appearance, the two cumbersome and clumsy beasts continued, one to graze and the other to browse. It was as if we were witnessing a scene from the beginning of time. In addition to this, as we returned to bed, there up the dry river bed, was a small herd of elephant — great, grey ghosts silently gliding across the sand to disappear in the forests on the edge of the floodplain. It was so beautiful and incredible that we did not even talk about it.

The different body shapes of the very large mammals are always incredible to me. The rhinoceros seems to be prehistoric in shape, with a boxed, squared-off look. In contrast, the hippopotamus, when seen out of the water, has a more rotund appearance, with rolls of flesh and silly, little, out-of-proportion legs.

A mother called Droopy

We accept that we should not interfere with the balance of nature and we respect nature's survival-of-the-fittest rule, but sometimes it is impossible not to become involved. We are all aware that when man interferes it is usually the animal or bird that subsequently suffers and has to be destroyed due to its altered behaviour, especially around humans. Strange how it is always the fault of the animal! Over the years we have attempted to provide homes for a few orphaned animals, but I had resolved never to try again, as frequently the outcome is so distressing.

Such resolutions are soon broken when an elephant is involved. Our feelings for the elephant are so strong that to make no attempt to help an elephant calf seemed to be not only unfeeling, but cruel. The drought years had taken their toll on the animals and many were in a very depressed physical condition. There had been one scraggy elephant cow in camp for about three days. She was accompanied by a young male, presumably her last-born, aged about ten. It was not usual for a cow elephant with a single companion to spend such a long time in camp, but we assumed that she was using the shelter afforded to rest and recover. She was in poor condition with a prominent pelvic girdle and a dry inelastic skin, as well as deep depressions above her eyes.

We called her Droopy and felt sure that she had recently aborted. There were still some nutritious albida pods around and although the rains had brought the first flush of grass through, this was not yet long enough to provide food. However, we attempt to grow a very small patch of grass around the house, mainly to keep down the dust. Droopy soon found this and each night came underneath the platform to graze. We were pleased that she could benefit from the fresh grass and hoped that she

An elephant mother and calf enjoying a mud bath, which should have been the shared experience of Droopy and her calf. The tenderness and concern displayed by elephant mothers is widely known and accepted, which makes Droopy's behaviour more difficult for me to understand.

would recover if the rains came. One morning, while sitting upstairs drinking our early morning tea, we checked the area with binoculars to see who was where and why. To our complete and utter surprise we saw Droopy appearing around the bend near the first hut accompanied by a very small, wobbly calf.

Hard to believe, but there it was, alive and well but still unsteady on its feet and falling over every few steps. As Droopy approached, we could see that she was still showing signs of birthing and her rear legs were stained with blood. The calf was hairy and his ears were very flat against his head. He stumbled about erratically and initially seemed to have difficulty finding his mother's teats, because she did not help by standing still with one leg forward, as the more experienced elephant cows do. Instead she was restless and constantly on the move. We kept very still so as not to frighten her or the calf and eventually she again came to feed right underneath the bedroom. The calf was so new and exhausted from the long walk that he frequently stayed down when he fell down. After a short sleep he would struggle up in a most ungainly fashion and seek comfort from being close to his mother. He walked rather like a drunk. In order to assist with balance, he spread his legs wide — sometimes so wide that they collapsed under him and he remained splayed out. After an hour or so, Droopy left us for the shelter of the trees and there she was joined by her older calf, who appeared to be quite terrified of the new youngster.

The day passed uneventfully. Droopy and her family were in sight until dark and that evening she returned to feed near the house. The calf mistakenly assumed that the rough cement

113

walls of our house were his mother's hide, so he rubbed up against them and fingered the chicken wire with his trunk. We were absolutely quiet and still inside the house, revelling in this close contact with a mother and calf. There is no doubt at all in my mind that the cow knew we were there. There were far too many scents and sounds for her to ignore. We assumed that she felt secure enough with us, not only to come herself, but also to bring her twelve hour old calf right up to our house. Eventually I could resist the temptation no longer, and when I saw that rubbery, out-of-control trunk reaching above the level

of the wall, I gently put out my hand and touched the calf. He immediately reacted as all newborns do, attempting to suckle my fingers and hand. His body hair was really spiky and reddish in colour and the texture of his skin was rubbery and moist. The skin on his ears was smooth and as I stroked him I was overcome. How could I be allowed to sit on the floor and fondle a totally wild elephant cow's newly born calf without causing her any distress or fear? Jeff, too, was full of emotion as he came to share the experience of touching the trunk, mouth and head of Droopy's baby.

When elephant calves are very young, their control of the trunk is non-existent, so they have to kneel down to drink. This is certainly not an efficient method and it makes them vulnerable to the ever-present threat from the larger predators who, on rare occasions, can manage to kill an elephant calf. This only occurs when a big group manages to isolate a calf from its mother, but most often elephant defend their young and lion are sometimes seen being chased off with their tails between their legs.

The formation of pans is attributed to the 'puddling' of a small depression which will hold water. The puddling is caused by the animals wallowing and compacting the mud. However, in certain circumstances, over-utilisation, particularly by large numbers of elephant, breaks the seal and so the pans no longer hold water. Over a period of time a small pool will become a pan, eventually reverting again to a small pool.

What makes us weep

The whole day had been an awesome experience, beyond my belief and expectation and the trust that she placed in us made me weep. She spent most of the night grazing and then browsing and we soon learnt to listen for the calf's recognition grumbles and also his growls when he was hungry. He didn't feed for long, five minutes on average, but did feed frequently and we went to bed filled with joy and wonder. During that night we heard the sound of prolonged elephant trumpeting. As there were many elephant in the area, we did not imagine it could be Droopy in distress.

Early the next morning, Jeff left to go to Mhangura, a six hour journey, and I prepared for the arrival of our sons and their friends. At about eight o'clock, Robert, the camp caretaker, came to me with the news that the baby elephant was going to die, as it was stuck in a hole. Together we hurried back to where the calf was suspended over a two metre deep gully, entangled in the roots and branches of the growth around the wash-away. There were signs that his mother had attempted to push him down or pull him up, but she could not work out which piece of root needed to be broken to release her calf and so she had left him.

One of his back legs was bent back on itself, he was dehydrated and quite terrified. As we approached he let out a series of high pitched squeals and thrashed around trying to free himself, but he was too weak. We worked out a plan to release him and went off to fetch ropes, saws and a wet sack, which we used to cool him down to relieve the effects of the dehydration. He was in such a turmoil that each time we approached he struggled more and more violently and I was sure that his screams of fear must attract his mother, as she

should not have been far away. It was now as hot as Hades, so we were working fast, but with one eye very definitely cocked to watch for the return of Droopy. We got the calf down to the bottom of the gulley, laid him in the shade and then covered him with the wet sack.

I did not attempt to feed him at that stage, as I thought that Droopy would return and be overjoyed to find that her calf was free again. After a few hours I realised that he could not last much longer without some nourishment, bearing in mind that he had fallen into the gulley during the night, so I decided to try to feed him. All we had was sterilised milk which I watered down, added some glucose and then tried to work out how I would actually get him to feed. This milk comes in very soft plastic bottles so, armed with a couple of these and a bucket full of the mix I set off, accompanied by Robert, who was to stand guard and watch out for the return of the elephant cow. I was amazed at how quickly a bond was established. At first the calf was uneasy when I attempted to handle and feed him, but after a few false starts he got the message and he would swallow as I squeezed. He drank about half a litre although there was a fair amount of spillage and, hoping that would be sufficient, I left him resting on his side under the shade of a tree.

The only reason I embarked on this attempt was because I was convinced that the mother would return. They are normally devoted and never abandon their young so quickly. More time went by with no sign of Droopy, so we prepared the second feed. To my delight, the calf now recognized me as a source of food and I was greeted with the welcome rumble and growl which I had heard the previous night. What joy!

116

Elephant have a regular routine, which is to bathe, to wallow and then to give themselves a dusting of 'talc'. Despite the thickness of their skins, they become irritated and suffer from biting flies. A layer of mud helps minimise the effects of bites. When Droopy's calf was dying, he was attacked, mainly around the eyes, by biting flies not much larger than a house fly, but with such a wicked bite that they constantly drew blood. We tried to ease his pain by putting damp towels over his eyes, as he was too weak to use his ears or trunk to brush the pests away.

It was now well after midday and my family were due to return, but being totally and utterly involved with the plight of the elephant calf, I had not given a thought to a meal for them. Loth to leave the elephant calf, I had to rush back to the kitchen and hastily sort out a snack.

When the boys arrived, I did not even ask how they were, what had happened with the exams or any of the normal parental questions. Instead I blurted out, 'Jeff, Droopy's baby had fallen in a gulley and its leg is hurt and I am trying to feed it and can you all help to carry it home?'
This they did and we settled into the routine of trying to feed him regularly with approximately the right amount of milk and we also tried to exercise him to make sure that he did not stay too long on one side for fear of compressing his lungs.

We carried him around in a tarpaulin as he was too weak to stumble more than a few steps, and we took turns to keep watch during the night to protect him against hyena or lion, but nothing came, not even his mother.

We battled on, but the inevitable occurred and the calf developed diarrhoea. I had no idea how to treat this. We increased the amount of glucose in his milk and gave him kaolin and morphine. Sadly it did not help and he died. Droopy returned four days later, but she was too late and I believe we were more distressed at his death than she. Maybe she was an indifferent mother or perhaps she knew there was another drought year ahead and that he would not survive as she was in poor condition and unable to nurture him.

During the drought years, malnutrition was widespread. There was one year when it was feared that the hippo population of the Zambezi Valley was infected with anthrax. The Luangwa Valley had experienced a violent outbreak of the disease the previous year and the spore lives forever it seems, and spreads over great distances. The days that year were punctuated by the reports from the men as they returned from their cruises, 'Another two carcases on Chikwenya Island', or, 'We had seventy crocs visual around the hippo carcase lodged below the hide.' For a short period everyone was panicky, particularly with regard to water, but the tests done by various vets associated with National Parks proved that the deaths were related to malnutrition and certainly not caused by an outbreak of anthrax.

Danger — keep out

The presence of a carcase in the river is guaranteed to reinforce the rule of not swimming, as it is uncanny where all the crocs come from and how fast they gather. Once, the helicopter pilot seconded to the anti-poaching unit visited and reported that he had just counted over one hundred and twenty crocs feeding on a hippo carcase about two kilometres upstream. The immediate reaction is that fantastic photographs can be obtained, but usually the water is so shallow and the sandbar so extensive, that you cannot get anywhere near the action and it is definitely not the right time to get out and push the boat!

Each year a number of crocodile farmers are given permits to collect eggs from specified areas in the valley and after five years or so they are required to return a percentage to designated areas which need to be restocked. This ensures the build-up of the crocodile population as, in the wild, such a small percentage of eggs grow and survive — other crocs, leguaan and catfish being the main predators.

The colouration of crocodiles varies considerably and, again, this is linked to habitat. Shallow, yellow sandbars usually mean that the crocodile population will be pale, while deep, dark waters produce almost black crocodiles. These adaptations are related to camouflage, with the crocodile being the master of the art.

Birds in brief

Below: *The anomaly of birds' common names always amazes me. Whitewinged black terns move through various stages of breeding dress before reaching mature colouration, only then appearing as whitewinged black terns.*

1) When viewed from the boat, the underparts of the whitefronted bee-eater are clearly visible and, once the birds settle and start feeding again, it is possible to get good feeding shots as they hawk for insects, in this case a bee.

The bird life in the Zambezi Valley is superb and we have a great diversity of species to observe and photograph, due to the combination of woodland and water habitats. For me, birds do not usually have such strong characters as mammals and for this reason I do not have many bird anecdotes. Their contribution however, is by no means insignificant, and for many folk, birds are the first attraction. Certainly bird watching and photography is very challenging, often frustrating, but in the end rewarding when one gets the perfect shot.

The fish eagle is probably the most spectacular of the eagles. Not only is his plumage very striking, but his call is wild, haunting and plaintive and just a little eerie as it peals across the river at dawn and dusk. We have a number of pairs

2) The pied kingfisher hovers for minutes on end while searching the shallows for suitably sized fish. Once the prey is selected, it plummets down into the water and, whether successful or not, returns to its habitual perch.

3) Greyhooded kingfishers huddle on the cold, winter mornings, not wanting to move until the sun has warmed not only them but also the insect life on which they prey. Not all kingfishers eat fish.

4) A fluke shutter speed allowed Jeff to record, in silhouette, a whitefronted bee-eater actually catching an insect.

5) Intricate and complicated weaving patterns are well illustrated in the design of this half constructed nest of the lesser masked weaver who has a bright, beady, yellow eye.

6) A lilacbreasted roller looking quizzical, and no doubt very confused, at the number of clicks and whirs from the cameras.

Right: *Perfect symmetry - the great white egret in flight. Caught on the down beat, the angle of the wings defines the primary feathers.*

of fish eagle along our riverbank and each year we try to monitor the breeding activity reasonably carefully.

A few years ago there was a scare on Lake Kariba, when it seemed that the eagles were suffering from the effects of excessive DDT. This insecticide had been used extensively for agricultural purposes and to control mosquitoes and tsetse fly. Recently its uncontrolled use has been discontinued, but, as it has a cumulative effect and lodges in the fatty tissue of humans, birds, beasts and fish, there may still be some danger. There are indications that the levels are still far too high. In

1) Bennet's woodpeckers frequently feed in the albidas, presumably because the wood is soft and the bark loose, enabling them to find a fair number of grubs and insects.

2) The threebanded courser's not-so-cryptic colours blend perfectly with the background soil near the red cliffs.

3) Few things are more dangerous to a leguaan than a martial eagle. Leguaan are the favoured prey of this most splendid bird, who can also take young monkey, baboon and even mongoose if it acts quickly enough.

4) Arguably the best groomed of the small raptors, the lizard buzzard sports a bow tie which, combined with his immaculate, light grey plumage, gives him an air of distinction.

5) The little bee-eater is the smallest of all the bee-eaters, but what a jewel. His mainly citrus colouration of yellow and limey-green is enhanced by the flash of blue eye shadow, present only in the adult bird.

6) The saddlebill stork literally stalks off with its prey – a squeaker caught in one of the small pans. Once away from the water, the birds bash the fish about before swallowing it headfirst.

7) Sacred ibis — surely the most spectacular of the ibis family — showing clearly, in flight, the blood-red veining which develops in the breeding season.

Left: Being the largest stork of all does not prevent a marabou from landing on an impossibly small branch. Along with the vulture it serves a very important role — that of cleaning up the remains of carcases.

birds, these high levels cause soft shells, which prevent the full development of the egg, causing a decline in the population. In some extreme cases in America and Europe, this has led to the disappearance of certain specialized feeders such as the osprey. Fortunately for us, it seems that the wholesale use of DDT was stopped in time for the fish eagle population not only to maintain itself, but also to increase in some areas.

The fish eagle is an aggressive bird and often we see an eagle attacking the slow-flying and vulnerable goliath heron. There is, inevitably, some competition as they both feed mainly on fish and often attempt to use the same stretch of water. This territorial competition seems to originate with the fish eagle; he is the one who swoops out of the clear skies like a cannonball and hits the goliath at his most vulnerable time, when he is becoming airborne, and the oh-so-slow wingbeats are becoming rhythmic and regular. It is not unlike a Spitfire

During the rainy season small terrace pans form and, as they dry up, the fishing birds such as yellowbilled storks, a.k.a. wood ibis, take advantage and feast on the trapped barbel (catfish). The still waters have allowed for excellent reflections and the birds appear, at first glance, to have legs quite out of proportion to their body size.

attacking a Heinkel and the end result is usually the same, as the slower bird is downed while the more athletic, speedy bird continues to fly high. Happily the goliath heron stalks his fish in shallow water, so when he gets bombed by the eagle he is safe from drowning, due to the combination of the shallow water and his long legs. He does take a hammering, however, and completely loses any semblance of dignity while trying to gain cover and dry his soggy plumage.

The lappetfaced vulture is the largest of them all, but certainly not the best looking, with creepy folds of pink skin around the head and neck. They are not very common in the valley and generally we see many more of the whitebacked and hooded vultures.

The redbilled quelea is an enemy of wheat and grain farmers throughout Africa. Quelea form flocks of millions. Once they are airborne, the entire flock moves as one and the disturbance created by millions of wingbeats raises dense dust clouds.

Overleaf: *Helmetted guinea fowl seek protection from predators at night and always roost, frequently in trees which have fallen down and have branches spreading over the water..*

A cast of characters

Respect is the key

There are many 'characters' who have enriched our lives during the years at Chikwenya. We have named these animals simply because it is easier to refer to any animal by a name rather than a number. They are not, nor have they ever been pets; nor are they tame. There is a degree of familiarity which has developed over the years and this acceptance has allowed us to approach closer than normal. In the main we have allowed them to take the initiative and make the approaches.

Therefore, certain behavioural traits can be observed at very close quarters, but all these animals are wild and will always be wild. People presume too much and become arrogant when dealing with wild animals. One of the most tragic and telling indications of today's values is the sign that has been put up at the entrance to Hwange National Park, 'You feed the animals and we shoot them'. Respect is the keyword. It is vital that consideration be shown for them as individual beasts and also as species which form an integral part of life in the valley. Intimate contact with wildlife and a personal observation of nature helps us in our self-discovery. The tendency is to anthropomorphise, but how else can interpretations of certain actions, reactions and vocalisations be made? Therefore, we include the main characters in our daily lives and actively seek them out at the beginning of each season. We concern ourselves when there is illness or even death amongst the 'residents' of Chikwenya and we make no apologies for this. This section serves to introduce the main characters and to relate some of the incidents or observations which have given us pleasure or caused us to weep or giggle or stay up all night wondering what the dawn will bring when one has heard the most horrendous noises and not been able to see who is attacking whom and what the outcome will be. Emotions do enter into it — it is impossible not to get involved to a degree, but we do strive to observe the code.

For me, the most regal of our antelope is the greater kudu. The males, even when not fully mature, carry beautifully spiralling horns, which, when they are in flight, are laid back and rest on either side of the hump behind the neck. This streamlined shape makes for greater speed through the heavy, riverine vegetation — their usual habitat.

The grand dame of Chikwenya

Without doubt, the most venerable and revered elephant in our area is a grand old dame called Chikwenya. She is an exceptionally respected matriarch and we believe that she is matriarch, not only of her immediate close family unit, but also of the entire clan living near Chikwenya in the valley. Jeff estimates that she is approximately fifty five years old. Certainly she has not got the rounded temples of the younger cows and her skin is loose and baggy, rather than tightly stretched. Her most distinguishing feature is one very long, perfectly straight tusk which reaches almost to the ground and it always appears to be clean and polished. At the moment, her immediate family unit consists of eleven beasts and she herself, despite her fairly advanced age, has a calf aged about two years.

We do not know enough about her group to be able to work out accurately which of the other calves belong to which cow.

The grand dame of Chikwenya, with her extended family, is not always easy to photograph. On this occasion, Jeff captured her on one of the grassy sandbars between the camp and Chikwenya Island. Her very long, slender, perfectly straight tusk makes her easy to recognise, even at a distance.

Even though she is one of the long-standing residents, she does not spend a great deal of time in camp. In fact her preferred feeding region is Chikwenya Island and we are frequently treated to the splendid sight of Chikwenya marshalling her family together in the early dawn. With fingers of mist swirling around the shadowy and indistinct river bank, she leads them without hesitation across the river, with short stops for the calves on the two small grassy islands. These crossings are always accompanied by a fair amount of noise and controlled excitement. It must be very daunting, when one is a young elephant calf, to be expected to follow the herd far and wide. To have to face the broad stretch of water, with its strongly flowing current, would be enough to reduce a human child to a quivering wreck, but the calves hesitate only briefly, and they sometimes hang onto their mothers' tails to stop themselves from being swept downstream.

Chikwenya and her family are always to be found when there is one of those conglomerations of elephant which occur infrequently during the months of August through to November. The greatest number of elephant seen together, immediately in front of the camp is eighty, but Jeff has seen in excess of a hundred cows and calves working their way through the *Vetevaria* at the extreme eastern end of our area. There they eventually congregated to water and wallow in one of the slower side channels. Unlike Hwange and Chobe, the Zambezi Valley is not known for its huge groups of elephant. In fact it is uncommon to see more than about ten elephant at a time and we are familiar with a number of the small family units and are usually able to gauge their reactions as far as vehicles and people are concerned.

Tuskless cows

One of the most tolerant and unflappable groups is that led by Agatha. She is a big, tuskless cow with a calf of about three years who appears to have inherited her mother's relaxed manner. Agatha's unit is small, only seven in total and except for one, each cow has a calf aged between one and five years. The cows are mainly tuskless, as are their calves, so obviously this trait is hereditary, rather like baldness. The only cow with tusks I have called Sabre Tooth. She has one thin, straight tusk and the stump of a second one, which has been broken close to her lip.

The youngest member of Agatha's family is the most appealing and plucky little calf now known as Twitchett. She is always delighted when they meet up with the other groups of cows and calves as she can then get down to the really serious business of playing endless games, interspersed with brief periods of rest enforced by her exhaustion, and also quick, snatch-and-grab type sucks at her mother's teats in passing. Frequently bowled over by the greetings of the bigger calves, she struggles to her feet again without hesitation and goes back for more. Such tenacity and determination to be shown by a baby! One day, I am sure she will be the matriarch of a large, extended family of elephants. I feel confident they will survive, if only due to the fact that there seems to be a definite tendency for the females in the valley to be tuskless and it is felt by a number of people that this change has been brought about by a form of natural selection to ensure the survival of the species. This theory is not based on any scientific evidence and is mere speculation. No ivory means no poachers and therefore survival, albeit in a modified form.

The three bulls

Among the big bulls who are frequently to be found at Chikwenya, there are three main stars. Saucer, the biggest of all the bulls, Little John, who is the most perfectly formed elephant that I have ever seen, and Big John.

Big John is the most adept at the practice of standing up on his hind legs to feed high and he did not deserve the indignity of having his photograph taken from the rear on one such occasion when everything was hanging loose, while he strived to achieve greater heights. Saucer was initially given the name of 'Flying Saucer', as he has a dish-shaped piece missing from his right ear and when we first came upon him, he would whirl, quick as a flash, and chase us with monotonous regularity and thoroughness! We enjoyed seeing him because he was such a huge specimen, but were always wary of him. His behaviour changed at the start of the 1989 season, when he came into camp in early April with a fairly large and deep hole in his rump caused by a tusk. The injury, we assumed, was caused by vigorous defence of his right to mate first with any receptive cow.

The fact that he was wounded caused us concern, as we felt he might become even more radical in his attitude towards humans, but this did not happen. He seemed to develop a moderate degree of tolerance and acceptance of us and the constant comings and goings which take place within the camp. That year was not a good year for him though, as despite the fairly rapid recovery from his puncture wound, some six months later he developed a badly infected foreleg. There was no wound apparent and we were at a loss to know what might have been the cause, but it became more and more swollen and was obviously extremely tender.

The more common picture of elephant in this feeding position is taken from the side. Big John, one of the Three Bulls, is here, caught in an unflattering pose, but for him it is a conventional occupation. He is a master of the art of standing up on his hind legs, in order to pull down the delectable fresh leaves and pods of the Acacia albidas. I speculate on how much effort is spent trying to lift the bulk of the head and trunk, and hold the position, when sometimes all that is gained is literally a handful of leaves.

Saucer, resting against the antheap near the house, demonstrates typical elephant behaviour, in that they often utilise slopes to assist in raising their enormous bodies from the prone position. They also have a rocking motion which seems to get them going initially. More often than not, they sleep on their feet, with their trunks relaxed and resting on the ground. Sometimes they snore.

Saucer suffered untold agonies, as he could not move except by dragging his forefoot and as it is impossible for an elephant to walk on three legs, he had to put his full weight on it just to proceed a few yards in search of food. Elephant require vast quantities of food, one hundred and fifty kilos a day of fresh mass, and it is also desirable that there is variety in the daily intake, so they have to cover vast distances to secure enough food to survive. Saucer was quite unable to do this and lost more and more weight and condition as the days went by. The infection also seemed to affect his balance and sense of direction and he would slowly move round and round in circles while half-heartedly browsing a few leaves in passing. One day, he painfully made his way through the dining area and down to the house, where he slowly lay down, resting against an antheap immediately in front of the ladder to our bedroom.

We watched him from afar and hoped that, having taken the weight and strain off his foot, he would be able to rest for a while. Little did we know that not only was he going to rest, but he was in fact going to sleep, and he slept soundly and well for almost an hour. Due to our close association with Saucer, I was becoming very concerned and felt sure that he had laid down to die. I could not see any sign of life. Jeff crept up closer and established that he was still breathing. The breaths came fast and shallow at first and then slowed down to what was almost a standstill, until he seemed close to death.

The passage of time was slow and nerve wracking for me and I deeply resented the comment from a guest, 'How are you going to move the body?' It was a valid and sensible question, but I could not bear the thought of Saucer dying. As if to prove us all fools, he suddenly lurched to his feet, using the slope of the termite mound for assistance, and stood in the shade for a few minutes. He then crossed the sandy river bed and went down to a protected bay full of water hyacinth. There he stayed for five hours with all four feet in the water, occasionally plucking at the odd hyacinth blossom. Dusk fell and Saucer was still bathing his swollen leg. At first light the next day, we were overjoyed to see him strolling up the path to the dining area in his usual confident fashion. He was still limping slightly and his foot was still swollen, but it was only a matter of time before he was back to normal and we were relieved.

I want to be alone

Fonda came into our lives in 1985. She was first seen by Jeff up at the airstrip and he reported a lioness who was not in very good condition, but who did not even deign to move when the vehicle passed by. She then appeared in the sandy river bed of the Sapi late that afternoon, literally strolling down to the water, utterly and supremely indifferent to our presence. She was not scrawny, but she was long and lean and probably hungry and I called her Fonda. There is always speculation when one sees a lioness on her own. Why is she not part of a pride? Obviously because she didn't want to be. She developed, over the years, into a truly formidable hunter and could tackle and bring down a mature cow buffalo on her own.

She often battled, as do all predators, and many hunts were unsuccessful, but she survived and became strong and more determined and, if possible, more aloof. She was never seen with any other lion except when she was in season and then she welcomed the attentions of all the males around. On one hilarious honeymoon, which took place right in front of our house, we all sat and watched while she mated with Blackbib who was then the dominant male. He was one of a trio whom we called The Three Musketeers.

As is so often the case, he became fatigued and relaxed momentarily, at which stage the second largest male called Red-beard approached. He and Blackbib had a fierce and dramatic fight batting each other viciously while standing on hind legs. Suddenly we saw Blondie, the youngest and smallest of the trio, slinking along the edge of the bank of the Sapi towards Fonda, who was waiting patiently for the victor to come and claim his spoils. She was not at all averse to allowing him to mate with her as well, albeit briefly. Out of

the corner of his eye, Blackbib caught sight of this intruder and, with a snarl of rage, rushed across the sand towards Blondie who 'snuk' off out of range with his tail between his legs. Despite the fairly continuous attentions from The Three Musketeers, Fonda did not become pregnant and we were convinced that she was a Queen.

134

Always stay in the hide

Fonda's indifference to humans almost caused me to have a heart attack on one occasion. I had taken two Australians to the hide near Grasshopper Creek and, on the way back to camp, passed Fonda; she was heading for Grasshopper Creek, so I felt that those particular guests would have an exciting time in the hide. In due course I went to pick them up for lunch and as I approached saw Fonda lying in the shade of a kigelia looking very round and full and licking her lips! I got nearer the hide and it was empty. Not a sign of the two Australians. For about thirty seconds I speculated as to whether she could have killed and eaten both of them! Then reason prevailed, sanity returned and I realized that Jeff had picked them up by boat on his return from a late morning cruise!

Opposite: All awash with gold, Fonda is seen in one of her favourite lookout places — on the edge of the terrace near Grasshopper Creek. In order to take advantage of any opportunity which may present itself, lion frequently lie up on a high level, ensuring good all round vision. Cheetah, too, are frequently seen on ant mounds, scanning the horizon before planning a hunt.

When she was in season, Fonda associated very willingly with all the males in the area. After this particular mating session with the Three Musketeers, she finally became pregnant, much to our delight. Like indulgent grand-parents, we had been waiting for years for something positive to happen.

Nomads

The Three Musketeers moved up towards Nyamepi, the camp in the national park, and we found ourselves with a new group of lions, again consisting of three young males. The dominant one in this group had a slight deformity on his right forefoot and he was christened Splayfoot. He was accompanied by a large, well-built lion of greyish colour, who had a lugubrious outlook and went under the name of Mournful and there was yet another Blondie. Again Fonda enjoyed the attentions of all three of them over a period of a couple of years and we were overjoyed to note that she was heavily pregnant when we returned to camp in March of 1988. She gave birth, in about the middle of May, to two cubs, but we did not see them for some weeks.

Early one morning, she brought them out into the open on the sandy river bed and we established that there was one male and one female. The female was inquisitive while the smaller

Boy and Girl greeting Blondie. It was scenes such as this that made us feel certain Blondie was the father of Fonda's cubs. Splayfoot and Mournful were still in the area, but whenever the cubs approached them, they moved off, sometimes cuffing the cubs on the way. By contrast, Blondie actually sought them out and he was very, very tolerant.

male was more timid. Having just read George Adamson's book, 'My Pride and Joy', we had no choice but to call them Boy and Girl. Fonda proved to be a devoted mother and was tireless in her efforts to provide food for the cubs and we were happy watching them grow, develop and thrive, close to us in the camp.

The same three males were still in the area and eventually we decided that Blondie must be the father, due to his tolerance of the cubs and his very protective manner towards them. They grew and gave up stalking the Land Rover and started to stalk game. In June 1989, tragedy struck and Splayfoot killed Boy by attacking him at the edge of a waterhole and drowning him. We were all distraught and grieved to watch Fonda and Girl wandering endlessly through the area, calling for Boy, but after a couple of days they accepted that he was gone and settled down.

The menacing stare of an angry lion definitely makes my hair stand on end and Splayfoot generally looked mean and nasty. His disposition did not endear him to us, especially after he had killed Boy. When he moved off to Nyamepi Camp, in Mana Pools National Park, I was very relieved.

All about survival

In some areas, it seems that there is a definite imbalance of the sexes and it is certain that there are many impala rams who never have the chance to mate due to this. Perhaps it was for the same reason that Splayfoot killed Boy when he was just thirteen months old. It must have been time for the young male to begin to mature sexually and as there was only one receptive female in the area with three mature males already competing for her favours, the presence of yet another fast maturing young male must have become too much of a threat for Splayfoot to accept. To us it seemed an extreme and unjustified action, but we were reacting with a human feeling of distaste and letting our emotions overrule our common sense. We cannot understand the strong urge of wild animals to procreate.

Girl was still very dependent on Fonda, but fate was working against them and in August, Fonda disappeared. We

Young lion can climb quite easily, but once fully grown, they become too heavy to be able to climb steep trunks. At this time, Girl was still very light and seemed to prefer to be up a tree. It gave her respite from the tsetse fly and also a good overview of what might be coming into range. Due to her somewhat inept hunting methods at first, her prey had to be quite close before she succeeded in killing it.

never found her body, but I feel sure that Splayfoot was responsible for her disappearance because she was still rejecting him and preferring the company of Girl. Splayfoot was an angry and aggressive lion.

This sad event left Girl entirely on her own, aged only fifteen months, and how she battled to survive! We were very tempted to help her by providing food, but managed to hold back and watched her cope with her 'Garboesque' lifestyle. She existed initially on baboon and became quite adept at climbing trees, presumably to spook them out. In time she graduated to killing impala, young waterbuck and young kudu. She too, has developed a strong, independent and very determined character and, like her mother, has chosen to remain alone. Other groups of lion have come through the area, but she has never joined them. However, the time is now ripe for her to start breeding and we think she has teamed up with a young nomadic male, who appears briefly from the other side of the Sapi and calls with a voice just like Blackbib and could be his son.

With the disappearance of Fonda, our nights became more peaceful but less atmospheric without her frequent and very distinctive calls. She never called without at least ten and often as many as thirty grunts and these were preceded by a long, extended, low preliminary call. When one becomes familiar with them, lion vocalisations are easy to distinguish, but I often ask myself whether the number of grunts has any special significance. Fonda had definite location calls with the cubs, as well as the come-and-get-it call and when she was in season, her voice procedure left nobody in any doubt as to what her status was, and certainly served to reinforce the attractive scents which she spread throughout her territory.

Wall to wall lion

In the latter months of the 1990 season, we had a brief, single visitation from a group of eleven lion. Fortunately it happened when there were no guests in camp as the escort duties that night would surely have been a fiasco. Everywhere we looked there were lion, mainly youngsters, who were totally indifferent to the spotlight. They came from the Sapi River, through the camp, and then went up towards the airstrip so maybe they were *jesse* lion. We can cope with one or two resident lion, but eleven of them lurking around would be just too much.

In the meantime, the eastern end of the area appears to have been colonised by a group of six lion known as The Demolition Squad, comprising one old male, Floppy Lip, one beautiful young male, Goldilocks, one strong, solid female, Butch, and three, as yet unnamed, younger females. The two males fought with ferocity for dominance and it would appear that Floppy Lip has now lost control of the pride to Goldilocks. Floppy Lip is tolerated, but has to keep on the outer perimeter of the group, and due to his injured jaw, really cannot kill at all, so is dependent on what the rest of them allow him to eat. I have little hope of his being there when we open camp next season; he is old, his teeth are blunt and he has definitely had a very active life, judging by his scars.

A new pride of lion appeared at the eastern end of our concession area. We now know that it is in fact the females who hold the territory on a long term basis; the pride males only serve for a couple of years before being eased out by the younger and fitter males, all needing to enjoy the opportunity of passing on their genes. Nature's rules are always reasonable and in particular that of the survival-of-the-fittest. When Floppy Lip, who was then the dominant male, was injured and lost the use of his lower jaw, he was no longer of any use to the pride, either as a hunter or as a protector, so he had to bow down and allow the strong male Goldilocks to move in and prove himself.

Bushbuck territory

Notch was a large and lovely looking male bushbuck, who had been in camp since we arrived at Chikwenya. Each year he became more at ease. He constantly fed on the lush, green mahogany leaves in the dining area and did a regular patrol round the kigelia trees when they were dropping their blossoms in August and September. Like all animals, he enjoyed the apple-ring pods of the albida trees and made daily visits to each tree. The camp environs were his territory, but he was no longer in his prime and there came a time when he was challenged by a younger and fitter ram. The fight was fierce and Notch came off second best with a large, deep, jagged hole in his rump caused by the sharp horn of his assailant. This did not heal well and he developed a huge abscess on his leg which should have been drained.

Each day he got thinner and thinner and could not walk more than a few steps without resting. He spent a lot of time lying down close to our house, in the dining area and near the radio room. This reinforces my thinking that often wounded animals come closer to human settlement for protection. The inevitable happened and we, or at least I, started to help him feed. I spent hours collecting bundles of leaves from the mahoganies and handfuls of albida pods and bunches of kigelia blooms and put them in a pile within easy reach of Notch. He would stagger to his feet and feed on the various goodies I collected. He became stronger and slowly recovered, but because I had provided for him, he was firmly and rightly convinced that I was the source of never-ending nourishment.

The staff willingly became involved in the salvation of Notch, and they too collected piles of his natural foods, placing these in convenient places for him, so that he did not need to leave the safety of the immediate camp area and again

Radio time was never dull when Notch was around, as he spent hours close by, waiting for the albida pods to fall from the trees above the radio room: extra rations were also available for him when we swept the roofs clean of pods and then he had a royal feast.

140

be challenged by the young ram. He recovered almost entirely, got back his good condition and had just a slight swelling and minor limp on his right rear leg. After his recovery, and as a result of the trust that had been built up between us, we spent a season of pure bliss with Notch behaving like a dog, following us around and sleeping close by. It was always amusing to watch the initial reaction from guests when they saw the shy, secretive bushbuck; they would become very silent and attempt a leopard-like crawl to get to within good photographic range, only to discover that we were all walking freely within half a metre of Notch, who had learnt trust. Leopard are very fond of bushbuck and, although we have no proof, we feel sure that Notch the bushbuck was killed by a leopard during the closed season of 1988. We still miss him.

The saga of Suzie

The other exceptional animal we have been lucky enough to observe regularly over a period of years was Suzie, who was a mature, female, black rhinoceros. The saga of Suzie really started one day in May, 1988. We have a mobile land hide which resembles a horsebox. Despite its appearance, it is very effective and we took two middle-aged English ladies to this hide after breakfast. They were a little nervous about being on their own in the bush, but we reassured them and off they went.

When it was time to collect them, near lunch hour, the guide driving the vehicle could not believe his eyes when he spotted a fully mature, female rhinoceros browsing within two metres of the hide. He waited a while, studying the rhino carefully, and then when she moved off he fetched the guests.

When we came to Chikwenya, National Parks policy did not permit the construction of any permanent hides and so Jeff evolved the mobile hide, which was built on a trailer and could be moved at will, depending on where there may or may not be good viewing opportunities. Each year the hides are revamped, along with the other vehicles. It was from this hide that the English ladies first saw Suzie.

They were almost speechless with fear. They had seen the rhino appear from out of the thicket and then, to their horror, she approached steadily closer and closer until she was feeding virtually underneath the supports of the hide! There were so scared that they turned their heads away, working on the premise if-I-can't-see-you-you-can't-see-me. Despite the truly amazing photographic opportunities they had, there is no record of this event, as they thought that the noise of the shutter clicking might provoke her into charging the hide.

Suzie was marvellous. She was very easy to distinguish as she had a really long, back horn. Over the years she became one of our regular bonuses. She was not at all aggressive nor was she nervous and in fact she did not display any of the normal black rhino characteristics. She spent many hours totally out in the open grasslands, chewing contentedly on weeds and when it was very hot and muggy, would plop herself into the remaining patch of water at Hammerkop Pool or Salvinia Pool and just lie and doze. She appeared to develop a genuine liking for our Land Rovers and would often walk steadily up to within half a metre of the front of the vehicle, sniff and then gently wander off.

As she became more and more habituated, we became increasingly concerned as she was very vulnerable out in the open. It would have been extremely easy to sight her from the Zambian bank, cross over by boat, kill her and head straight back again. We thought long and hard and eventually approached National Parks to suggest that they try to translocate her to a safer area. She was also particularly vulnerable due to the size of her horn. The day came when the capture unit arrived, but despite an extensive search they failed to find her. She must have gone well back into the *jesse* and did not reappear for some days, by which time the capture unit had moved on. So we, and many of our guests, continued to enjoy the evenings with Suzie on the floodplain in the setting sun and rising moon, looking so right and happy. At the end of the 1988 season, our final evening was spent watching the full moon rise with a shadowy Suzie silhouetted in the last rays of the sun, totally at peace.

The closed season that year seemed interminable. We worried about Suzie and also Fonda and her cubs. With jubilation, Jeff reported seeing Suzie in April of the following year. However, that was the last time she was seen and we fear that she was shot by poachers, as there was a large group operating up the Sapi beyond the airstrip and they killed five rhino. So who knows for sure what happened to Suzie?

In 1989 there were only two sightings of rhino and in 1990 we did not see any rhino at all, although there is still fresh spoor of two males as well as a cow and calf. They definitely lurk in the *jesse* and only venture out at night to water. They have most certainly learned to fear.

Bush bovines

Most of the year we have small groups of elderly buffalo bulls, who are very much 'in residence'. They have been eased out of the breeding herds and form a type of Old School Tie association. Long hours are spent lying in the sandy river bed of the Sapi in the blazing sun. They then plod down to the river's edge and wallow for a short while, before taking up a position very close to my path home. There they lie, in amongst the clumps of *Vetevaria* and ruminate for hours.

A few years ago we had a simply splendid specimen of buffalo with a huge spread of horns, but minus his tail. Inevitably he became known as Stumpy, and most mornings we would wake up to the sight of Stumpy slowly and painfully

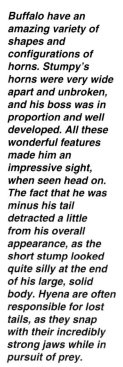

Buffalo have an amazing variety of shapes and configurations of horns. Stumpy's horns were very wide apart and unbroken, and his boss was in proportion and well developed. All these wonderful features made him an impressive sight, when seen head on. The fact that he was minus his tail detracted a little from his overall appearance, as the short stump looked quite silly at the end of his large, solid body. Hyena are often responsible for lost tails, as they snap with their incredibly strong jaws while in pursuit of prey.

getting to his feet and trying to rid his old bones of the stiffness. His head was very definitely a trophy hunter's dream and regrettably we got to measure it when he was killed by The Three Musketeers on the opposite side of the Sapi River. Buffalo snort and snuffle and when distressed, they moo and low. Late one night we heard the all too familiar sounds of a buffalo being killed. The volume of the sound decreased gradually after some fifteen minutes, which meant that the lion, despite there being three of them, had taken quarter of an hour to kill Stumpy. He provided a very good meal, not only for The Three Musketeers, but also for Fonda and both her cubs. It is always very distressing to hear the gradually diminishing sounds of a beast in the last throes, but he was an old specimen well past his heyday.

Although Fonda did not participate in the death of the black rhino calf, she was not averse to sharing the carcase when the Three Musketeers had had their fill. We forgave her this transgression because, at that time, she was still feeding her cubs.

Easy prey

The Three Musketeers really disgraced themselves and fell totally out of favour one September day when they killed a rhino calf aged about fifteen months. The timing was unfortunate, their choice of prey was unfortunate and their *modus operandi* was extremely unfortunate. There was an upsurge of poaching in our immediate area at that time and we were very much on the alert for anything at all suspicious. When we found the headless body of a young rhino in the river terrace, our first and very natural reaction was that poachers were responsible. Frantic messages to the National Parks anti-poaching unit resulted in a hectic drive by them from Nyamepi, their headquarters. They gave strict instructions not to go too near, nor to spoil the spoor, nor to compromise the exercise in any way.

The game drives and cruises had to proceed, so I had the task of escorting the patrol of scouts to the scene of the crime. We were all very alert and we slowly approached close to the foul smelling headless carcase, by vehicle. At first everyone was convinced that it was a poached animal, but in the middle of scouting around for spoor or tracks of any sort, there was a series of very menacing growls from the adrenalin grass and out bounded The Three Musketeers. They had killed the calf and then removed the head, but in an extremely clean fashion, and left the remainder of the kill to mature in the hot September sun. Why they chose to kill one of our precious rhino nobody knows, except of course that all predators are opportunists and black rhino calves are more than usually vulnerable because of their odd habit of walking in front of their mothers. In this case, the ambush was a huge success. In addition to the fact that they had fed well, they had also caused a state of uproar to prevail in the area by their strange and somewhat macabre behaviour.

Sir Harry, the hippo

There was a hippo called Harry. In fact he was and is called Sir Harry, after a well-known English gentleman who visits us fairly often. The river is full of hippos and many a canoeist has found the whirls and swirls of dirty water, which are generally the only indicators of their presence, to be somewhat unnerving. They grunt, and pop up occasionally right in front of the canoe with a surprised exhalation! Sir Harry is a loner and, we assume, male. He lives very close to camp and gingers up the drowsy guests on the afternoon cruises by refusing to move out of the channel so that the boats are forced to pass close by. Harry has developed a tendency to almost leap out of the water with enthusiasm in the late evening, with his jaws stretched just as wide as they possibly can be. This is always guaranteed to create a feeling of unmitigated terror at the size of the gape and the length of the tusks.

In spite of his displays, Harry is benign and he has come to accept our presence, as well as that of our smelly boats. I suppose he has little choice, as to move would necessitate gaining a new territory, and the demands of the younger and more aggressive bulls are obviously more urgent and compulsive than his own.

Sir Harry — pretending to be fierce and often succeeding in causing a ripple, not only in the water, but also in the equilibrium of the guests returning from an afternoon cruise, which should be calm and peaceful and good for the soul.

Overleaf: The best of Chikwenya. Albida woodland bathed in the late afternoon light, against a bullet blue sky.

145

No city lights

It seems that this is indeed a film set, carefully arranged, but not so. Familiarity with the area, and the inhabitants' routines, not to mention the time of year (to take into account the movements of the sun), all combine to make such photographic opportunities easily available.

Right: Girl, in repose on a branch, taking advantage of the additional height to improve her chances of success in the hunt. Most hunts seem to occur in the twilight hours — through dawn and at dusk. Predator's vision is one hundred percent at night, whereas that of the prey animals is not quite as sharp.

Bush telegraph

At Chikwenya we try to eliminate reminders of our guests' normal pressured lifestyles. We have no radios, TVs, VCRs, or tape decks and definitely no newspapers. News of importance comes by word of mouth. We try to encourage our guests to become part of our 'capsule' and allow themselves to benefit from the rhythm of nature.

Light is one of the special characteristics of Chikwenya. Life takes place under the sun and the moon and the stars. We use a generator for a very short time each evening, attempting to live in harmony with our natural surroundings as far as possible. In most areas of camp life this philosophy works extremely well and our guests soon fall under Chikwenya's magical spell, but it is the lack of lights which they often find the most difficult aspect to accept and adapt to.

'Lights out'

Very many amusing tales of the camp result from our 'lights out' policy. We certainly have no city lights at Chikwenya. At the end of the day, when it is time to turn off the generator and allow the quiet of the wilderness to permeate our hearing we often, unwittingly, cause some distress to our guests. There was once a lady who virtually attacked Jeff early one morning. 'Do you know what you made me do?' she demanded. 'No', replied a mystified Jeff. 'You turned the lights out after just three minutes, not five, as promised, and by mistake I swallowed my contact lens!' It seemed that she had used both the drinking glasses in the bathroom. One for water with which to take some medication, and one with water in which rested her contact lenses. Luckily, only one lens went down the hatch. The second was recovered next morning from the water remaining in the glass!

A similar incident, but with not quite such serious consequences, occurred when a guest ended up with his toothbrush in his ear instead of his mouth! He said that he was poised for the first stroke when, yet again, the lights went out before time. The sudden darkness disturbed his aim and he had to spend a few minutes trying to wipe the toothpaste out of his ear. Some explanation for these two stories is necessary. When we do the escort duties to the huts at night, the guide on duty generally says, 'I'll turn the lights out in five minutes.' This is absolutely true for the folk staying in the huts at the beginning of the patrol. However, by the time the guests who live in Hut Number 8 get dropped off, the time factor has reduced considerably and they are lucky if they get two or three minutes before darkness descends. The moral of the story has to be, light your candle immediately!

The reluctant cook

I have never aspired to any great level of achievement in the culinary field. In fact one of my recurring nightmares is having the chef get too sick to cook. This did happen once. We were still newcomers to Chikwenya, the camp was full and I was on the verge of hysteria. I immediately got onto the radio in an attempt to procure the services of a replacement, but without success. I resorted to threats and stated categorically, and in my most determined radio voice, 'I cannot and will not cook,' but still no relief. Salvation came in the form of Mattias, who was then a kitchen porter. He handled most of the basics and I prevailed upon the cook to make a pudding quickly before we shipped him off to hospital. He had malaria so the training programme took place in his more lucid moments on the way to the airstrip!

Chikwenya airstrip is carved out of the jesse. For newcomers to Africa and the wilds, it must be a daunting sight. The camp is so well hidden that few visitors get a glimpse of any building from the air and the airstrip appears very isolated.

150

Running repairs

Jeff has a great sense of the dramatic, which becomes evident when he is telling a tale or recounting the day's experiences. In order to provide a balancing factor, I tend to become more pragmatic as the years go by. I have also learned not to worry when he does not return on time. His method of dealing with and fixing any given problem is never orthodox, and not always permanent, but he usually manages to get back without abandoning either the vehicle or the boat!

There was a time in late September when he was more than usually late for breakfast. The stomach rumbles towards the end of a morning cruise or drive or walk usually emanate from Jeff and not an elephant! It was getting hot as midday approached, but eventually the boat came into sight, still under power and there was no waving of life-jackets to attract

the island, to reach the colony. All was well. A superb performance from the birds, as well as from a leguaan who was preying not only on the eggs, but also on the young fledglings. It had made for a happy crew, well satisfied with what the day had provided so far.

They had just commenced the return journey to camp when there was an almighty crunch. The trimaran lurched violently to one side and then came to an abrupt halt. The cause quickly became apparent. Due to the changing levels in the river, stumps are sometimes exposed and visible. At other times they lurk just below the surface, ready to inflict mortal injuries to fibreglass canoe hulls and there was a large, well weathered and very pointy stump protruding right through the floor of the left hand hull! Inevitably all hell broke loose.

Among birders, the breeding colonies of carmine bee-eaters hold a great attraction and we are fortunate in having one upstream of camp in the channel. The carmines are migratory, arriving in the Zambezi Valley in August and leaving in April, having bred here.

A water monitor, a.k.a. leguaan, is a ferocious and persistent predator of the fledglings as well as the eggs of the carmine bee-eaters. They are frequently seen along the riverbanks and utilise the empty breeding tunnels of these birds.

attention or call for assistance. The cruise had been intended specifically to cater for photographers who wanted to get good flight and feeding shots of the carmine bee-eaters. They had bumbled along downstream around the end of Chikwenya Island and then upstream through the channel which dissects

There was immediate panic from the passengers, with many and varied instructions being given by Jeff. Order was eventually restored when it became clear the boat was not going to sink. Certainly there was water in the boat, but the stump was serving as a plug, allowing just a small amount to seep in.

The next step was to work out a method of getting the considerable combined weight of boat and bodies off the stump. This was not easy, as there was about five metres of water beneath the boat and in that water, at that time of year, large and particularly active crocodiles were living! Jeff tends to carry an enormous amount of assorted equipment with him, both in the Land Rover and on the boat, but as an axe and a hacksaw were not part of the boat kit, he had to gradually chip away at the stump with his sheath knife. This took time, but eventually the bulk of it had been cut away, as had the edge of the knife.

The master plan had then to be put into effect. Everyone moved to the extreme right of the boat, in this way reducing the pressure on the left hand hull. Jeff, together with a couple of other fearless guests, went overboard and by dint of much heaving, whilst balanced on bits of stump, they managed to lever the boat off. The hole was now wide open, allowing huge volumes of water to rush in. The flood was stopped by stuffing a towel into the hole and then placing the large concrete anchor over the towel and the hole! This novel arrangement slowed the flow of water sufficiently to allow the boat to proceed gingerly back to camp in time for lunch. There had to be a use for that large concrete anchor. It certainly wasn't the normal one of holding the boat, as once thrown overboard it was impossible to retrieve without mechanical assistance. Just another variation on the theme of imaginative excuses for being late for a meal!

The afternoon cruise boat is on its return journey to camp, with a small family group of elephant at ease on the bank of Grasshopper Creek.

I'm sorry, but ...

On the subject of excuses, there are many and varied tales which are told by guides throughout the country when they return to camp late for meals. It would indeed be a perfect world if we could instantly conjure up freshly prepared food but that is not possible. There has to be some sort of set time for meals. Visitors get more than usually hungry having spent hours out in the open and really enjoy their meals taken under the shade of the giant mahogany tree. The chef enjoys preparing good wholesome meals. He is gratified when all is eaten with relish, but trying to keep food fresh and ready to eat when it is being cooked and kept warm on an uncontrollable open wood fire is no mean feat.

This small area of conflict certainly encourages the guides to come up with new, and if possible, ever more colourful stories than those used on the previous day. One such occasion sticks in my mind, not for its originality, but for the fact that the guide had quite forgotten that I also organise the schedule of game viewing activities. When he came in half an hour behind time, with a sheepish expression on his face and launched into a story of how many punctures he had had and how the jack was not working, he was totally deflated when I reminded him gently that he had been on a cruise!

Be prepared!

Jeff was very innovative and could effect repairs with somewhat unorthodox materials and in his own eccentric fashion. This lack of finesse gave rise to his nickname, 'Captain Hammer', as his philosophy was, 'When in doubt, give it a clout!' I often used to shudder when I heard guests asking Jeff for help with their delicate, computerised automatic cameras.

The specific incident I am leading to, was in my opinion, Jeff's ultimate effort. It was September and he was cruising with a boat full of overseas guests. The objective was the photography of bee-eaters, but at the critical stage of trying to hold the boat steady against the current, the engine stopped. Amidst much gesticulating and shouting of instructions to all on board, Jeff managed to find the cause of the trouble. A reinforced rubber ring had broken. He fiddled for a while in his tool box, but no suitable replacement came to hand. Looking around, he asked if any guest had a strong rubber band. No luck. The idea of abandoning the cruise and walking back to the camp was mooted, but not well received. Salvation came in the form of a condom, somewhat diffidently offered. Jeff saw the possibilities and proceeded to doctor it with his sheath knife. It was duly fitted to shrieks of laughter and the cruise came to a successful conclusion.

That night we drank to the guest for being prepared and to Jeff for being prepared to 'give it a go'! The sequel to this incident came in March the following year when all the equipment was being overhauled. The mechanic who stripped that outboard motor was amused when he discovered what had been used to repair the throttle mechanism and even more so when Jeff told him to leave it, as he had been given to understand it was made of heavy duty, superior material and should last a long time!

153

Sometimes we cheat

Another of Jeff's quirks is his penchant for the 'perfect take', and this is particularly true with regard to the fish eagle. Heaven only knows how many rolls of film have been used over the years, not only by Jeff, but by hundreds of bemused guests, all of whom are instructed and encouraged to take shot after shot after shot, as the majestic eagle flies in and out of the frame while engaged in his daily task of swooping down to pick up the small fish floating on the surface of the river which are thrown there by Jeff to encourage just this feat.

Many people 'feed' the eagles and it is incredible how quickly the eagle accept this manna from heaven. Equally quickly they accept that it comes to a halt at the end of the November each year, hopefully to recommence in the following April. Fish eagle are spectacular due to the amazing speed and dexterity which they display when the fish become visible. One of our guests was so enthralled with the whole stage-managed performance that she ignored the advice given and did not focus on the bird as he made his approach and dive. A couple of weeks after her return to America, we received a card in which was enclosed a print of the most perfect splash. The colour was good and strong and the definition was superb. What a pity there was no sign of any bird, nor of any fish for that matter, just the perfectly focussed splash!

The fish eagle scenario

Having sighted its prey, the fish eagle takes off from his perch on the river bank.

The moment before the 'take', he thrusts his legs and claws forward, inches from the surface of the river.

Success! Although he is not hunting as such, we marvel at the accuracy of his strike.

Having secured the fish, the eagle flies off to a favoured perch on the mainland to feed in peace.

Hearing is believing

One day, we had a visitor who was determined to learn everything possible on her first safari. She diligently copied down in a notebook every word that Jeff said. On occasions, he used to mumble into his beard and guests were hard-pressed to hear anything at all, let alone hear with any degree of accuracy.

This fact was illustrated when we read her notes that evening. She had recorded seeing a 'dog-nosed duck'. In vain we tried to explain that it had been a 'knob-nosed duck'. She refused to accept our word as she implicitly believed every word of wisdom from the 'Great White Wotsit'.

Lingua franca

People who have English as their mother tongue are, as a rule, notoriously lazy about making any effort to speak other languages and we are no exception. When we have European guests whose English vocabulary is limited the conversations tend to become rather stilted and misunderstandings can and do occur. A classic example comes to mind. A guest from Europe had booked to be with us for some days. He was particularly anxious to get good portrait photographs of water-buck. At first we did not consider this to be a problem but his camera equipment was very limited. Not only was it limited but it lived, securely tied up, in a large and very crackly plastic bag. Luckily there were no other guests in camp, so all efforts could be directed towards achieving this goal.

Like his methods of repairing things, Jeff's methods of photography are unusual. He often shoots straight into the sun and deliberately looks for backlight. The more conventional photographer wants the light to be shining towards the subject. Having approached the waterbuck more closely than usual in order to accommodate the limited range of the guest's camera, and having carefully lined up the Land Rover with fantastic atmospheric backlight illustrating so beautifully the very furry coats of the beasts, Jeff was totally unbelieving when, at this late stage, he heard loud and prolonged crackles as the camera was removed from its plastic bag. The light was still good, but by the time everything was arranged to the satisfaction of the guest, sign language being used, Jeff was amazed to be told, 'Too dark'. Another angle of approach was tried, with different light being thrown on the subject, but this was, 'Too light'. They continued the quest for the perfect waterbuck photograph, undeterred and undaunted. They did not always get within range. Sometimes, even the very tolerant waterbuck turned tail and fled, disturbed by the combination of crackles and the stream of muttered curses and then it was, 'Too far'.

As an alternative Jeff decided that he would approach from the river. This is not generally as effective with waterbuck, but certainly worth a try. He left with the hopeful guest sitting in solitary state in the front seat of *Nkwazi*. A couple of hours went by and I was down at the edge of the river watching the always splendid sunset, waiting to welcome them back. Jeff

got out, as did our one and only guest, with not a word being exchanged! This stony silence continued whilst we had a drink round the camp fire.

When we got home Jeff exploded with pent-up rage and frustration. It seemed that the afternoon's exercise had not been a success. The waterbuck, once again, fled just as the craft hove into view. Jeff thought that perhaps he could offer something different, in the form of the whitefronted bee-eaters and their nesting tunnels. As he could normally

Looking very cuddly on a winter morning, a young waterbuck pauses momentarily in her grazing along the Sapi bank. The fluffy coats of waterbuck give a soft silhouette, which is very distinctive, as most of our other antelope are smooth and sleek.

approach to within one metre of them, if everyone was quiet and sat still, he was confident that some photographic success would be achieved.

All did go well until the guest demanded that he 'Switch Off', whereupon Jeff gave up. It is not easy to manoeuvre the very wide craft through the fallen trees, which lie close to the birds' nesting holes, without inflicting damage. Once in place and in order to allow time to focus you have to hold the boat against the current, all the time watching for the light and keeping the angle right. The current runs at about five knots so the engine has to be kept running steadily, and with a bit of juggling you can in fact, 'stop', adjacent to the birds. However, not with the best will in the world can one 'Switch off', and thus avoid the very slight vibrations caused by the motor running. Jeff's refusal to switch-off had angered the guest, who felt Jeff was being uncooperative. The request angered Jeff, as he now felt that they had no common ground. This meant he had failed and failure is never easy to accept. By the end of the day I had managed to smooth the ruffled brows but all this could have been avoided if we had been able to speak each other's language. Do elephants who live in different countries have the same problem? Of course not! Rumbles are universal.

In the past, the bulk of our guests have come from either America or England, but recently there has been an increase in the number of European visitors. In 1990, for the first time, we had a group of Italians. We were a little concerned, as previous experience had given us cause to believe that the Latins were inclined to be rather noisy, due to their excitable and exuberant temperaments. The only consolation was that there were no other guests in camp and so any disturbance would come from someone within the group. We waited and wondered if we would be able to communicate properly with them.

So often, due to the lack of a common language, the visitors from European countries do not get the full benefit of the safari, which is intended to be not just a game drive or cruise, but also a learning experience with explanations from the guides as to who does what, to whom, and when, and who eats whom, where. Fortunately our fears were totally unfounded. Most of the group spoke really good English and their courier was to hand, if needed. A great time was had by all; good game, good birds, good photographs and very good spirits.

A young waterbuck ram provided Jeff with what he considered to be the perfect portrait.

There's a branch in my soup

The Latins are always much more expressive than those of English descent and spontaneous songs became the order of the day, especially on the cruises. The combination of the savage colours of the sunsets, accentuated by the smoke haze, with the exultant voices of the Italians was most pleasing. All conversation around the camp fire was abandoned in favour of songs and the volume increased as the evening progressed, as did our appreciation of their naturally musical and tuneful voices. Eventually it was time for dinner, which was disrupted in a most unusual manner. A large and substantial branch fell into the soup! Our dining area is not covered and the 'roof' consists of branches intertwined with vines and creepers. We blamed the Italians' operatic fervour for the disintegration of the roof, but in fact it was due to wood borers and termites.

The guests behaved in an exemplary fashion and were undeterred by this extra-curricular event. We brushed off the worst of the debris and then continued dinner, albeit with eyes and ears on full alert for the next creak or crack. We had so enjoyed their singing that we decided to try to show them that we were not entirely unmusical. After dinner the entire staff congregated behind the bar and they entertained our guests with their fantastically rich, harmonising voices. They are able to stand unselfconsciously and, without any assistance from instruments, burst into song and carry a true tune. I could not help but wonder what the game was thinking! Once a pattern has been established it should be constant and this night's sounds were definitely a departure from the normal murmurings around the campfire.

Hunting at Grasshopper Creek

During our first year at Chikwenya we named certain areas for their salient features and Grasshopper Creek was then a most inviting little waterway into which we could drive the boat. We were short of fresh food and hoped to catch some fish. Having no worms, I was tasked with the procurement of bait in the form of grasshoppers. This may sound easy, but it certainly proved not to be so. First of all you have to take into consideration the type of grasshopper, not all of them are palatable or acceptable. Furthermore, the soft skins of the abdomens of a hopper do not retain the insides very well, so care has to be taken not to bash them too hard. One cannot tempt bream with a hook baited only with prickly grasshopper legs, they simply must have the choice of a bite at the body as well.

Grasshopper catching is specialized and the most effective weapon is a leafy twig, which stuns but does not squash them. Once the method has been mastered, the next trick is to locate the temporarily stunned insect which has fallen into a thick, high patch of grass.

My best bag was six grasshoppers in two hours. Using these Jeff caught a grand total of two squeakers, which we do not eat. Squeakers, or grunters as they are often called, are a member of the catfish family and their looks are against them. Revolting whiskers sprout from their jaws. They are slimy all over and the fins are not only extremely sharp, but also poisonous. If a barb breaks off and lodges in a finger, a most unpleasant reaction tends to develop, which inevitably requires medical attention. As if this is not enough, the fish squeaks or grunts when caught and handled. No wonder we do not eat them!

The big five myth

We accept that we are part of the 'use it or lose it' policy and we assist, in a very small way, by bringing about a greater degree of understanding and tolerance in our guests. We endeavour to slow them down, if only temporarily, and we also try very hard to dispel 'The Big Five Myth'. Some safari operators aim for impact in the form of close-up contacts and photographs of elephant, rhino, buffalo, lion and leopard. These animals are known as 'The Big Five'. This originated from the safari hunters and relates not only to the size of the trophy head, but also to the degree of difficulty and the danger element. The term has spread to the photographic safari operators, as an objective for the less informed visitor.

At Chikwenya we also place emphasis on birds, insects, flowers, grasses, dung and debris. The amazing variety keeps us constantly stimulated and somewhat embarrassed at our lack of accurate information. Probably the most rewarding aspect of being a safari guide is the repeat guest. We have one who came initially for two days, secondly for a week, thirdly for two weeks and finally for a full month. Her range of interests has, over the years, expanded greatly. Now she is a true amateur naturalist and conservationist, as well as being a good friend and part of our family. It is achievements such as this that give one the self-control to deal with the checklist mentality of some guests. Once we had a visitor, who, having watched a female black rhino approach to within two metres of the front of the Land Rover, allowing unrivalled opportunities for observation and photography, turned round and asked, 'What else is there?' Where have the values gone and what can we do to redress this lack of empathy?

1) Aeschynomene fluitens, the yellow water pea, is one of the many aquatic plants seen while cruising on the Zambezi River. Growing along the banks, its tendrils reach into the mainstram.

2) The spiky red blossoms of the flame combretum, Combretum microphyllum, provide a perfect illustration of the common name, as the growth pattern resembles tiny, flickering flames.

3) Emerging from its cocoon during the rainy season, this speckled emperor moth is seen on the ground, where its dominant false eyes are clearly visible. These features are designed to confuse predators.

4) While driving in the albida woodland, we are treated to the sight of contorted trunks and sinuous growth forms. Theses are the vines. The most spectacular is the Combretum microphyllum.

5) A deeper understanding of the wilderness grows in us when we stop quietly to glimpse and wonder at such beautiful cameos. This abstract work of art is delicate, intricate and yet very practical. Spider's webs have a purpose; they catch the prey.

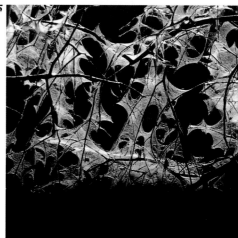

The 'people' business

Having been in the 'people' business for many years, we have noticed the numerous and varied reactions and behaviour patterns which emerge. Some of the traits are common, no matter where people come from, or what type of lifestyle they lead. Everyone loves the young of the animal world and we all have an atavistic streak which urges us to continue to watch when a predator is hunting or actually killing its prey. Many people, we find, feel the need to put themselves into a potentially dangerous position, just to get the adrenalin going again. It would seem that the controls which prevail in the 'civilised' world have been more than successful and thus the need to 'prove oneself' becomes paramount when visiting less developed areas. The tragedy of this warped thinking is that often it is the animal which has to be destroyed, as a result of the selfish and mindless behaviour of a sensation seeker.

Arguably the greatest disappointment for the overseas visitor is the realisation that Africa is not the harsh, cruel, menacing continent that it is made out to be. More often than not, the various species co-exist very peacefully with due regard and consideration for the needs of other individuals and other species. Indeed, one would be hard pressed to find anywhere, more evidence of caring behaviour than that exhibited by the individual animals in a family unit of elephant. They are simply the best, and without flogging an already dead horse, I wonder why we aren't more like them?

The fact that our concession area is part of the Sapi Safari Area, which is a controlled hunting area, does inevitably raise a few perennial thorny issues. Whilst we personally, do not feel the need to shoot and kill, various mitigating factors must be taken into consideration. The hunting safari business is a huge earner of foreign currency, which is vital to the development of Zimbabwe.

Furthermore, the professional hunters who regularly track on foot, are, like us, a deterrent to the poachers and the continued presence of hunters in the more remote, hard-to-patrol areas is an advantage which benefits anti-poaching measures. The operation of hunting safaris in the communal lands is now becoming more common and this is of specific benefit to the residents of these communal lands. We have a CAMPFIRE (Communal Areas Management Plan For Indigenous Resources) programme, which actively encourages the development of hunting safaris rather than half-hearted cultivation or keeping of livestock in the marginal lands and the direct benefits to the community as a whole are quite considerable.

This form of utilisation ensures the survival of game, as it now has a monetary value to the rural population of the area. For them, this aspect is the one of importance. It is unrealistic to expect folk who are hungry, seeking education and betterment, to appreciate the aesthetic values of the elephant which has just destroyed their entire maize crop. Likewise, the value in monetary terms of a trophy lion sold to a hunter, can go a long way towards replacing a few scrawny cattle or goats. An additional benefit is in nutrition. The meat from the hunts belongs to the community and malnutrition, due to lack of protein, can be reduced and eventually eliminated. Finally, by protecting the game, the rural population become active conservationists, even unwittingly. They no longer give aid and assistance to the poachers, as has often been the case in the past.

One of our tuskless cows and her immediate family, feeding in a relaxed manner. The young calf is still wobbly and unsure of itself, but ready to play games and already attempting to follow the leader!

Paradise

One of the few irritations I experience are the questions, well meaning no doubt, 'Don't you get bored?' or, 'Aren't you lonely?' On average we meet in the region of seven hundred and fifty guests each season. Meeting such a number of people in a nine month period, there is little chance of being lonely or bored. It is beyond my comprehension how one could get bored with the incredible variety of human characters and with the wealth of the natural resource available to us. It could be said that we live in a paradise and we are happy to share it with those who seek us out.

Chikwenya draws visitors from all walks of life and from all age groups. Our upper age limit to date is an eighty two year old Englishman travelling with his eighty year old sister.

Their visit was one of the highlights of that season. Despite their vintage, neither of them was going to waste any of their safari time, but on one occasion the fellow took matters to extremes when he woke up at two thirty in the morning, washed and dressed and shaved! Then he proceeded next door to wake up his sister, insisting that it was five thirty and that they should be ready and waiting for their morning safari. The eighty year old lady's vision was apparently more acute as she took a brief look at her clock, realised it was two thirty in the morning and sent her older brother back to bed with, I believe, a somewhat acerbic comment about geriatrics, and instructions to be careful of the lion that had been in camp earlier!

Although we have lived for many years in the Zambezi valley, it was only at Chikwenya that we became aware of kudu habitually congregating on antheaps. Whether this is protective behaviour, or whether the height provides a better lookout, we can only guess. The redbilled oxpeckers serve a purpose; that of removing ticks and other pests, but they are also a great irritant to the host animal at times, especially when they peck at the delicate areas.

Walk, don't run

Sitting round the camp fire in the dark listening to the night sounds is the time to relate 'lion stories'. They always seem to have more impact when it is dark. This also helps us to condition people to go to bed early! Guests feel so much safer when tucked up under a mosquito net. One evening we were discussing how to behave when meeting a lion on foot. As with everything, there is a right way and a wrong way. The right thing to do is not to panic, do not run, just walk slowly backwards. Predators get very excited by any sudden movement and running could encourage them to give chase.

Having set out the guidelines, I immediately disgraced myself the very next day, by running when I came face to face with a lion just past Hut Number 3. Happily, that lion reacted in the same way. We were both walking fast and almost bumped into each other as the lion came up over the bank of the Sapi. It was my first eyeball to eyeball confrontation with a lion on my own and I scuttled back to the shelter of the hut, risking one glance backwards to see where the lion was. Much to my relief, it too was fleeing back across the Sapi at high speed. This experience allows me to relate extremely sympathetically to the lady guest who, at about midday, saw a large lioness walking right in front of her hut. The couple had only just arrived in camp and been given the usual warnings about the presence of animals. Her husband had made his way to the dining area and was happily quaffing his first beer. Some time passed and she did not appear, so we decided to check up to see if she had lost her way. We found her standing on the loo seat, with a toothmug of neat gin in her hand, pointing in the direction that the lion had gone. We had no difficulty getting them to bed early that night.

Fonda was indifferent to humans, but was always aware of us. She tolerated our presence, but was, first and last, a hunter.

Why are we scared?

I do not believe that any modern human can smell fear, but most certainly all animals, and possibly people who are still living in pure primitive conditions do so and react accordingly. It is not just that one breaks out into a sweat, because this we also do when we are very hot. There is definitely something else, and it is sometimes so strong that it becomes almost tangible, even though you actually cannot smell it. How sad it is that the inhabitants of our chosen area can evoke such an extreme reaction from the rare visitor who simply cannot relate, in any way, to the wild.

The tragedy of such unfounded fear is that never do the mammals or reptiles deliberately set out to kill or maim us. Their actions and reactions are essentially those of an animal following the course which instinct dictates to ensure the survival and safety of not only the animal in question, but the dependent family unit and the species as a whole.

Sometimes one of our guests has been more than usually nervous. Our philosophy has been to introduce nervous people gradually to the object they fear and not to push them into any situation which could cause them a complete and utter breakdown.

My own pet aversion is spiders — large hairy spiders — and I do not enjoy the period just after the first rains when we have a positive glut of them hatching out. Most of these are *solifugae,* also known incorrectly as hunting spiders, who rush to and fro frantically seeking food, and causing a few hiccups to the equilibrium of myself and some of our guests. The spider menace is short lived, but we always have frogs and we love them. They are tree frogs and congregate in the cisterns and other strategic places from which they take advantage of the numbers of insects which are attracted to the lights. They are a great help in reducing the population of mossies and other undesirables and, along with the gheckos, they are protected. We indoctrinate our guests, willingly or otherwise, and courses of frog appreciation regularly take place.

There was a time when the presence of tree frogs in the toilet area caused a fairly major disruption to the tranquility of the camp. We had turned the generator off and gone to bed. Jeff was gently snoring when I heard an almighty scream from the direction of Hut Number 1. It was blood curdling, ear splitting and repeated a few times with increasing intensity. I leapt up, shook Jeff awake, handed him his gun and shoved him down the ladder to go and check on the problem. All this took a few minutes to accomplish, especially as he had to find his boots first and lace them up well! Just as he was thoroughly prepared, poised for action and ready to leap to the rescue there came another voice from the camp area. This time it was a male voice which said, with a strong transatlantic accent, 'It's only a frog'. With her small penlight torch, the poor lady had attempted to answer the call of nature during the night and had flattened a beautiful alabaster white tree frog sitting on the white loo seat.

This young male lion is just beginning to look as if he could present a potential threat, but is still young enough to enjoy climbing trees and flexing his muscles. All part of growing up.

Reptiles unlimited

Some years the frog population takes a dive. Bats are the most to blame, with snakes running second as they too devour a goodly number of our frogs. The sharp, high-pitched squeak which one hears during the night, followed by a loud slurping and smacking sound, is a clear indication that the bats are enjoying their night-time feast. Their eating habits are nothing less than revolting. The sound effects have to be heard to be believed and, as a final touch, they disembowel their prey and discard the entrails all over the unsuspecting sleeper below.

Fortunately, the mossie nets usually take the brunt of the debris, yet another reason for regularly climbing into, what one of our American guests referred to as, 'cones of celibacy'. His contention was that *it* would be a lot easier in a canoe than in one of the Chikwenya beds with its tightly tucked in mosquito net. Mossie nets are an acquired taste, certainly, but it is amazing what a sense of security one gets from being under a net when sleeping out in the open. I believe it is the billowing, white, unnatural shape that deters the game from approaching too close and Jeff will never go without his.

There are other 'residents' of the area who colonise the storerooms and bins, creating 'housekeeping hazards' for the bush camp. Rodents are plentiful, particularly if we have had a good rainy season, and many hours are spent setting up rat-traps on shelves in the storeroom. Most of the time this area is poorly lit, so I often set them off by standing on the shelves, thus risking the loss of a toe as well as tetanus! The presence of rats in the storeroom encourages their natural predators to move in, so then we not only have the rats and traps to deal with, but we also have to avoid the odd snake.

We have here a somewhat macabre illustration of a spotted bush snake eating a tree frog — favoured prey — in my office.

Radio relays

One year I instructed the caretaker staff, by radio, to do some basic stocktaking so that I could order stores before coming back into camp. The arrangement was that the staff would relay back the figures half an hour later. The time came and I called and called until I was blue in the face. Eventually a somewhat garbled message came over the air. It appeared that they could not count because there was a Mozambique spitting cobra in the storeroom. What were they to do?

Two things gave us pleasure and a sense of achievement. Firstly, the staff had not just killed the snake without question, which would have been a normal reaction, and secondly they had identified the snake. In the beginning we had spent time with our staff, trying to persuade them not just to kill on sight. They now check as to the type of snake first, and assess the danger, or lack of danger, before lashing out with a huge stick.

Another radio message which gave us a sense of achievement came from the cook, reporting storm damage to the roof of the storeroom. The radio was crackly and it was not easy to 'read'. Suddenly I realised that he was saying, 'The *Acacia albida* branch has broken the roof of the store'. It would have been a lot easier for him to have said 'a tree', but we do try to refer to the trees and shrubs by their correct botanical names, and it is good that the staff too, have picked up the habit.

Live and let live

Among the evergreen trees all around the camp, there are a number of boomslangs and vine snakes. Both are back-fanged and neither is aggressive, but they are venomous. It addition to these two species we have a really good population of harmless spotted bush snakes. To the uninitiated they are easy to confuse. Once, late at night, our waiter killed a snake and the next morning he brought it to us for identification. We got out the book and showed him that it was, in fact, only a spotted bush snake and not a boomslang nor a vine snake. He then gently picked it up by the tail and walked off saying, 'Sorry, my friend, but it was dark.'

But, back to the rodents — the most appealing and the most destructive of them is the dormouse. They really make a meal of it, so much so, that when I found one desperately swimming round and round the bowl of the toilet, I was tempted to kill it immediately, but I found that I could not. Not after it had spent the whole night swimming in ever decreasing circles and still survived. I called on one of the guides to do the foul deed, but he also found the task too daunting. Not only did he rescue the dormouse from the water, but he dried it off and made a little nest in his top pocket where it could warm up before he released it! This act of mercy took place just the day after I had discovered that rats and mice had chewed their way through a number of our best reference books and, in retrospect, I question my sanity.

The flying boat

One of the most romantic visitors to Chikwenya was the Catalina. This Second World War vintage aircraft has been adapted for use as a novel form of transport for tourists by a flamboyant Frenchman. The Catalina is capable of landing on both land and water, but the thrill of landing on water far outweighs the conventional aircraft landings and he has designed a series of trips which utilise most of the large stretches of water in Africa from the Nile down to the Zambezi, visiting *en route* all the Rift Valley lakes. This is travel as it should be, fantastic, slow and gracious.

There were some anxious moments prior to the Catalina's arrival, as this was the first time she had landed on the middle Zambezi. We wondered whether the water was really deep enough. Jeff plumbed the channel and laid a series of markers for the pilot to follow to avoid the worst of the sandbars. We waited expectantly for her appearance and all normal work came to a standstill as we watched the overfly, the approach and finally the landing, which was made in a great fountain of spray.

The resident game appeared to be totally unperturbed by this new noise. The engines have a deeper drone than the normal aircraft used in the valley, but it was an acceptable noise. The Old Daga Boys, grazing on the small grass island opposite the landing zone, barely lifted their heads, and the elephant continued to drink and enjoy their mudbaths while the Catalina taxied down to camp. Perhaps the fact that it is such a venerable aircraft contributes to the feeling of romance, as well as the fact that it can land on all the most remote rivers and lakes in Africa, thus joining the ranks of the explorers.

She moored opposite the camp and her passengers enjoyed a few days of game viewing and photography. The sight of her squatting in the moonlight, amongst the pods of hippo was unusual, but not at all out of place, as she really seemed to belong there. Although we did not get a chance to actually fly in her, even climbing all over the structure was exciting. With regret we watched as she taxied slowly upstream, doing battle with the sandbars as the river level had dropped to an all-time low.

I know that we all wished we could drop everything and fly away on this romantic, nostalgic adventure. Once in position the engines revved up, the speed increased and eventually her wide, low slung belly lifted off the surface of the water and she flew away, looking for all the world like an albatross.

A Second World War vintage Catalina flying boat could be considered out of place in the wilderness, but seen here at sunset, moored on the river opposite camp, she merely added to the romance.

Overleaf: A natural inhabitant, also seen at sunset, one of the Daga Boys steadily chomps his way along the river bank.

168

Looking forward

Policies practised in Zimbabwe with regard to the conservation, preservation and protection of the nation's invaluable wildlife heritage are far-sighted and courageous. The level of dedication to the ideal is gratifying and I believe the richness and diversity of our lives in the Zambezi Valley is ensured for the present, although our lives are not important. What is important and vital is commitment to the continuing long term preservation of wilderness areas.

Many potential threats loom on the horizon. There is the possibility of an additional dam planned for Mupata Gorge, to provide yet more power to the developing nation. Exploration for oil has begun, which to the present time has been carried out in a sensitive manner, but if the results give positive indications, it may lead to full scale drilling and oil production in the valley. Extended tsetse control operations could lead to the invasion of the valley by domestic stock. There has been expansion of tourist facilities into the valley as a whole and into the Mana Pools National Park.

The protection of wilderness resources is essential. Development plans should be given serious consideration by the public, as well as by Government, before irrevocable steps are taken which may result in permanent damage, if not total destruction, of delicate and fragile ecosystems. The priceless inheritance belongs to all Zimbabweans; ours to cherish and conserve for future generations, not only of the human race, but of elephant, rhino, impala and honey badgers.

Very recently, there have been alarming and well-publicised examples of the deadly dangers against which some species are struggling for survival. Horrendous damage has already been done to the black rhinoceros population by poachers, encouraged by high prices offered for their grisly wares.

We have been involved in the plight of these vulnerable creatures. In 1984 the estimated number of black rhino in the lower Zambezi Valley was 1150. A detailed study made in 1988 showed that some 600 black rhino had been killed since 1984. By 1989 the estimated popluation was reduced to 700, with a mere 467 individuals identified during aerial survey. Therefore their number is down by around 450, taking into account an assumed growth rate of six per cent on the numbers previously recorded, less the numbers killed and captured. That this has happened so quickly is incredible. That it has taken place with the whole world looking on, with countrywide and worldwide campaigns backing efforts to protect the rhino is even more distressing.

Efforts to redress the situation have been made. Breeding nuclei have been established inside the country on private farms and number just under 200 beasts. Captive breeding units outside Zimbabwe are also being established with fourteen animals contributed by this country. The objective is to increase the number of beasts to 40.

The survival of the black rhino is topical and newsworthy, but it is only one part of the greater question of survival of wildlife areas. Our presence in such areas should, in the main, continue to be passive and our attitude, considerate and caring. We must try to accommodate the needs of modern day man so he will learn to consider the wilderness worthy of his concern. I believe that wild and beautiful places will become more revered in the future and pray that Chikwenya will always be there for our children's children to explore and delight in, as we have done.

Suzie represents the best; a viable, strong population of black rhinoceros, living in their natural habitat. This has been decimated to the point where extinction is a very real possibility. There is a chance that the population may recover and we must endeavour to protect them and their rightful place effectively.

Epilogue

Jeffery Stutchbury died of cancer on the 4th of April 1992, aged sixty five. His family were at his bedside. His last wish was to return to Chikwenya and the valley. His illness prevented it.

The following are extracted from letters of condolences to the family.

Jeff Stutchbury was a man of the wild, someone who understood nature and her ways so deeply that he could offer the rest of us insights into his particular corner of Africa in a way that was reminiscent of the early explorers. He was the last of a dying breed.

We are privileged, those of us who were introduced to one of the last wild parts of the earth by Jeffery Stutchbury. We saw with his eyes, learned from his store of wisdom and shared his boundless enthusiasm, a part of the world that we must preserve. He gave us back our heritage, sharply etched by his wisdom, and showed us things that we take for granted. We learned patience, long hours in one of his hides at the waters' edge and its reward, a leopard, lithe in the golden afternoon light, coming down to drink. We found out what matters and what does not, and how to recognise the two.

He had a style, a presence, the ability to hold your attention for hours, and to impart his pleasure and wonder in the Zambezi Valley freshly minted with each new day. He was uncompromising, overbearing, impossible, irresistibly charming and unforgettable.

Jeff, that larger than life personality who devoted his life to nurturing and preserving all of nature's creations and he inspired in all who knew him a love of all things natural.

Jeff was a lion of a man. Brave, kind, creative, a warm laughing family man, independent, unbeatable except by death. A loyal and unselfish friend.

He lived life to the full, was never idle, left his print on many a guide and inspired literally thousands of people throughout the world. He was the best known wildlife character in Africa's recent times.

From him I began to understand, to appreciate and to learn. A comment softly spoken, a gesture widely made, a wild and angry tirade. But always the magic that was his, that lit the bush, that fired the soul. Soft, touch not the tree, let it grow, let it be. But always, even as I miss Africa, he is there. I will not scar a tree, will not break a plant, and will always leave that which I find as it should be. I will learn, feel, and understand, and only because I have been taught. And it is to my teacher that I now bear tribute.

He was a rare type of person - a great independent spirit - he did what he wanted to do and lived a life he always wanted - to live in Africa in the wild - photographing wildlife.

This aristocratic kudu bull is a symbol of everything we hold precious and revere.

We remember his endless enthusiasm and deep affection for the valley. We are eternally indebted to him for 'infecting' us with that same love about everything Zambezi, especially Chikwenya.

Jeff was a respected and dedicated conservationist and wildlife expert who served our country well. He has left a proud legacy and we have all benefited from from his knowledge and understanding of our natural environment.

Jeff's love of the bush was wonderful to behold, and to feel, and inevitably, to share, for it was most gloriously infectious. We think of his complete communion with his trees, grasses, animals, birds and insects, water, sunrises and sunsets.

There aren't many people in this world who have the soul deep love for nature as Jeff did. It shone from everything he said and did.

Jeff's passing is in many ways the end of an era — the last of the giants.

Stutchbury looked too good to be true, an identikit of the old African hero. He was tall and lean and bronzed, with one of those magnificent dark blond curling beards that had

Rider Haggard rhapsodising about battle axes in the dawn of the world. He will live on in the hearts and minds of those who met him, and in the ears of those avid to hear campfire talk of him — and there will be many.

I met Jeff when I was 24, he taught me that freedom, self value, commitment and dreams were more important than money. Jeff has always carried my respect and is to me the Gandhi of the wildlife world. Very few people have had the strength of character to do what they have wanted to do and in this world of grey people, he has been a teacher and is very, very special.

No one who ever met him will ever forget Jeff. He became a legend in his own time. A gentle man, a gentleman, an eccentric and a total individual.

Being with him — on the Lake, at Water Wilderness, and lastly driving amongst those magnificent albida groves at Chikwenya, walking through the adrenalin grass, or on his beloved *Nkwazi* was a magical experience that I feel incredibly lucky to have shared with him. His schoolboy excitement was contagious then, as always, and will long be remembered by all who loved him and revelled in his company.

Whenever I hear the call of the fish eagle, in my memory I shall envisage Jeff, at the helm, calling to them and awaiting their reply.

I valued him as a good friend, almost a brother, and as a committed and dedicated fellow conservationist. I also admired his individulaity and eccentricty. He was a great character, reminiscent of someone from the first Elizabethan age — an idealist and adventurer.

So gentle and kindly disposed with a great sense of humour.

Memories and sorrows cause our tears to drop if we meditate our manager who left us without 'goodbye' you are still in our mind, rest in peace and God be with you in the Garden of Eden.

He taught us so much and opened our senses to so much more than they had ever been exposed to before.

'You worked side by side helping and supporting each other. You shared the wild places and the wild creatures. You went together for peace and revitalisation into the beautiful wilderness. You both marvelled at the wonder and balance of nature. You gazed at night at the universe's diadem of stars.'